ULTIMATE HISTORY TAKEDOWN

An Epic 625-Question Quiz Battle Across the Ages

ROBIN WHY

Contents

A QUICK INTRODUCTION 8
THE ANCIENT WORLD **10**
MYSTERIOUS ORIGINS AND ANCIENT PUZZLES 11
    The Dawn of Humanity 12
    Early Human History 17
    The Origins of Language 22
    Megalithic Traces 27
    The Birth of Agriculture and Civilization 32
THE LOST KINGDOMS OF ANTIQUITY 37
    The Rise and Fall of African Powers 38
    Middle East – Masters of Metal and Builders of Empire 43
    Secrets of the Americas 49
    The First European Civilizations 54
    Roman Oddities 59
MEDIEVAL AND RENAISSANCE ENIGMAS **64**
THE DARK AGES – MYTHS, LEGENDS AND UNKNOWN HEROES .. 65
    The Aftermath of Rome 66
    Conquest and Combat 71
    Plagues and Cures 76
    The Viking Discoveries 81
    Religious Upheavals 86
THE RENAISSANCE AND BEYOND – THE RISE OF THE CURIOUS . 92
    The Hidden Lives of Peasants 93
    The Seven Seas 98
    Patronage and the Power of Art 103
    Intellectual Movements and Secret Societies 109
    The Age of Exploration 114

For all the history buffs, trivia titans and budding factologists

Disclaimer

This book is intended for informational and entertainment purposes only. While every effort has been made to ensure the accuracy and reliability of the content at the time of publication, the author and publisher make no representations or warranties regarding the completeness, correctness, or current relevance of the information presented. Historical facts and interpretations may vary over time and among sources.

This book may include references to events, people, or cultural practices that are subject to debate or differing perspectives. Any opinions or interpretations expressed are those of the author and are not intended to offend or misrepresent.

The publisher and author disclaim any liability for any loss or damage incurred as a direct or indirect result of the use of or reliance on the material in this book.

All trademarks, product names, or images mentioned belong to their respective owners and are used for identification or historical reference purposes only.

Polite Note to the Reader

This book is written in US English except where fidelity to other languages or accents are appropriate.

Copyright © Robin Why 2025

All rights reserved

ISBN: 9798286008285

HIDDEN HISTORIES THAT SHAPED THE WORLD 120

INDUSTRIAL REVOLUTION – THE STEAM POWERED ERA 121

- The Birth of Innovation – How Tech Reshaped the World 122
- Rebels Against the Machine 127
- Scientific Oddities – The Bizarre Beliefs of the Past 133
- The Hidden Costs of Progress – Pollution and Peril 138
- Railroads and the Race Against Time 144

WORLD WAR WEIRDNESS & COLD WAR CONSPIRACIES 150

- Curiosities of the Great War 151
- The Strangest Secrets of World War II 156
- The Forgotten Frontiers – Revolutions and Resistance 161
- The Hidden Aftermath of WWII 166
- Beyond the Cuban Missile Crisis 171

MODERN MAYHEM & 20TH CENTURY TWISTS 178

POP CULTURE & POLITICAL PUZZLES 179

- Strange & Surprising Stories in Modern History 180
- Hollywood vs. History – Dubious "Historical" Movies 185
- The Power of Music and Youth Culture 190
- Soviet Union – The World's Most Unexpected Breakup 195
- Future Predictions, Paradoxes, and Doomsdays 201

FINAL SHOWDOWN 206

- Final Words: The Never-Ending Puzzle of History 237

About the Author 241

More Books by Robin Why 242

Free Trivia Audiobook 246

Get yours at WWW.ROBINWHY.COM

A QUICK INTRODUCTION

Welcome to the Time Traveler's Trivia Takedown

Can You Handle the Hardest History Trivia Challenge Ever?

Welcome, history buff. You're about to embark on a one-of-a-kind challenge—a test of intellect, memory, and curiosity. This is not just another history book. It's a trivia battleground, where your knowledge will be put to the test, and history itself will be your greatest opponent. You think you know the past? Prepare to be surprised during this ultimate battle of wits through time!

Every page of this book will push you to think differently about history. We're going beyond dates and names. We'll uncover the bizarre, the overlooked, and the truly mind-blowing moments that have shaped human civilization. These challenging Trivia Takedown quizzes designed to separate the casual fan from the true history gladiators.

History isn't just about the past—it's the story of how we got here. And the more we learn, the more we realize how little we truly know.

- Who really discovered America first? Spoiler: It probably wasn't Columbus.
- What ancient civilization had flushing toilets before Rome was even a thing?

Knowing these details doesn't just make you a better trivia player—it helps you understand the world in a whole new way.

How to Use This Book

This book is structured as a progressive challenge, taking you through different eras in history.

- Each chapter has questions that focus on a specific time period and covers some of the most fascinating, unexpected, and challenging aspects of that era.

- At the end of each chapter, you'll find the answers as well as some extra knowledge nuggets to give context to these fascinating facts.

- Keep score as you go! Compete against yourself, challenge friends, or use this as an educational tool. Remember—if your scores are low don't fret—at least you're learning something new!

So, let's begin our journey where it all started: the dawn of humanity.

THE ANCIENT WORLD

MYSTERIOUS ORIGINS AND ANCIENT PUZZLES

Welcome to the dawn of everything—a time before kings and empires, before writing and wheels, when survival meant outsmarting saber-toothed predators and mastering the mysteries of fire. This chapter is your passport to the wild frontiers of prehistory, where ancient humans roamed vast landscapes, braved colossal climate shifts, and left tantalizing traces of their existence carved in stone, buried in caves, and even encoded in our very DNA. We'll explore how our species emerged from the depths of time, crossed continents, and sparked the great adventure of human history. Prepare to be amazed by our earliest ancestors, whose legacies still live within us, and marvel at the ingenuity of early humans who crafted tools, kindled flames, and began to shape the world.

But it's not just about bones and stones—it's about the great human puzzle that continues to intrigue scientists and explorers alike. How did our ancestors survive cataclysmic volcanic winters? Why did they paint mysterious symbols on cave walls or bury their dead with flowers? From the enigmatic origins of language to the birth of agriculture and the rise of the first great monuments, this chapter uncovers the twists and turns of our earliest days.

Did you know...?

Our ancestors may have evolved large brains not just for survival, but for social survival. The "social brain hypothesis" suggests that navigating complex relationships, alliances, and communication was a powerful evolutionary pressure. Gossip, empathy, and even humor may have had more survival value than brute strength—pushing the evolution of language, memory, and emotional intelligence as key human traits.

The Dawn of Humanity

The story of humanity is a tale of survival, adaptation, and mystery. How much do you really know about our ancient origins?

1. Which human ancestor is believed to have first used fire regularly?
   a) Homo habilis
   b) Australopithecus sediba
   c) Homo erectus
   d) Homo sapiens idaltu

2. Which extinct human species interbred with modern humans, leaving genetic traces in our DNA?
   a) Neanderthals
   b) Homo habilis
   c) Homo erectus
   d) Australopithecus

3. What's the estimated age of the earliest known Homo sapien fossils?
   a) 50,000 years
   b) 120,000 years
   c) 300,000 years
   d) 1 million years

4. Which of the following human relatives was initially discovered through DNA evidence?
   a) Denisovans
   b) Homo naledi
   c) Neanderthals
   d) Homo floresiensis

5. What major climate event may have nearly wiped out early human populations?
   a) The Little Ice Age
   b) The eruption of Mount Toba
   c) The Younger Dryas cold snap
   d) The Great Drought

6. Which group of early humans is nicknamed "the hobbits" due to their small size?
   a) Homo erectus
   b) Neanderthals
   c) Homo floresiensis
   d) Denisovans

7. What surprising discovery was made about Homo floresiensis?
   a) It may have coexisted with modern humans as recently as 12,000 years ago
   b) It used writing
   c) It had six fingers on each hand
   d) It lived in the Arctic

8. Around how long ago did humans first begin migrating out of Africa?
   a) 200,000 years
   b) 60,000 years
   c) 10,000 years
   d) 500,000 years

9. What is the name of the land bridge that connected Siberia to North America during the Ice Age?
   a) Beringia
   b) Pangea
   c) Gondwana
   d) Atlantis

10. Which of these hominins is known to have interbred with both modern humans and Neanderthals?
    a) Homo ergaster
    b) Australopithecus garhi
    c) Denisovans
    d) Homo rudolfensis

11. What unusual evidence suggests Neanderthals may have practiced some form of burial or ritual behavior?
a) Cave paintings
b) Tools made of metal
c) Deliberately buried remains with flowers
d) Written symbols on bones

12. What major adaptation allowed early humans to develop complex societies?
a) The ability to digest milk as adults
b) The invention of agriculture
c) The discovery of bronze
d) Domestication of horses

13. What is the scientific term for the period when Homo sapiens and other human species coexisted?
a) The Paleolithic Era
b) The Holocene Epoch
c) The Pleistocene Epoch
d) The Neolithic Revolution

14. What African site contains some of the oldest known evidence of early human activity?
a) Olduvai Gorge
b) Lascaux Cave
c) Göbekli Tepe
d) The Great Rift Valley

15. True or False: All modern humans can trace their ancestry to a single population that lived in Africa.

ANSWERS

1. **b) Africa** – The oldest known Homo sapiens fossils, found in Morocco, date back around 300,000 years. DNA evidence also strongly supports an African origin.

2. **a) Neanderthals** – Many modern humans, especially of European and Asian descent, carry Neanderthal DNA, meaning our ancestors interbred with them.

3. **c) 300,000 years** – Fossils from Morocco indicate Homo sapiens existed at least that long ago, reshaping previous theories.

4. **a) Denisovans** – Unlike Neanderthals, Denisovans were first identified in 2010 through DNA extracted from a finger bone fossil in Siberia. Later, their genetic legacy was found in modern human populations.

5. **b) The eruption of Mount Toba** – About 74,000 years ago, this super volcano erupted, triggering a dramatic climate shift that may have pushed early human populations to the brink of extinction.

6. **c) Homo floresiensis** – These small-statured humans, found in Indonesia, earned the nickname "hobbits" because of their tiny size (around 3.5 feet tall).

7. **a) It may have coexisted with modern humans as recently as 50,000 years ago** – *Homo floresiensis*, discovered in Indonesia, may have lived until surprisingly recently, overlapping with modern humans. Their small size (~1 meter tall) led to the nickname "hobbit."

8. **b) 60,000 years** – While small migrations may have occurred earlier, most scientists agree that large-scale migration out of Africa took place around this time.

9. **a) Beringia** – This land bridge between Siberia and Alaska allowed early humans to reach the Americas.

10. **c) Denisovans** – Genetic evidence shows Denisovans interbred with both Neanderthals and modern *Homo sapiens*, creating a fascinating web of human ancestry.

11. **c) Deliberately buried remains with flowers** – Some Neanderthal burial sites suggest ritualistic behavior, indicating they may have had spiritual beliefs.

12. **b) The invention of agriculture** – Farming led to permanent settlements, which in turn allowed for the rise of complex societies.

13. **c) The Pleistocene Epoch** – This was the Ice Age period when multiple human species coexisted, including Neanderthals, Denisovans, and Homo sapiens.

14. **a) Olduvai Gorge** – Located in Tanzania, this site has yielded some of the oldest known human fossils and tools.

15. **True** – Genetic studies confirm that all modern humans can trace their ancestry to a common population in Africa.

Early Human History

Human history didn't begin with written records—it started long before, with the first stone tools, early art, and the development of new ways to survive. How much do you know about the earliest innovations of our ancestors?

1. What is the oldest known tool-making tradition, dating back around 2.6 million years?
   a) Acheulean
   b) Mousterian
   c) Oldowan
   d) Clovis

2. What material did early humans use to create some of the first-ever tools?
   a) Bronze
   b) Bone
   c) Iron
   d) Stone

3. Where were the earliest known cave paintings discovered?
   a) France
   b) Spain
   c) Indonesia
   d) South Africa

4. Which species is believed to have created the earliest known cave paintings, dating back over 64,000 years?
   a) Homo erectus
   b) Homo sapiens
   c) Neanderthals
   d) Denisovans

5. What prehistoric period is known for the first widespread use of metal tools?
   a) The Neolithic Era
   b) The Copper Age
   c) The Iron Age
   d) The Bronze Age

6. What key innovation separated the Neolithic (New Stone Age) from earlier prehistoric periods?
   a) The use of fire
   b) The development of agriculture
   c) The invention of pottery
   d) Domestication of the dog

7. Which site contains the oldest known intentional human burial, dating to about 100,000 years ago?
   a) La Ferrassie, France
   b) Qafzeh Cave, Israel
   c) Shanidar Cave, Iraq
   d) Sima de los Huesos, Spain

8. What is the earliest known musical instrument?
   a) Bone flute
   b) Drum made of animal skin
   c) Wooden xylophone
   d) Shell trumpet

9. What was one of the primary reasons early humans developed sewing and clothing?
   a) To protect against the cold during Ice Age periods
   b) To display social status
   c) To improve hunting camouflage
   d) For religious ceremonies

10. What ancient carving, created over 30,000 years ago, is one of the oldest known depictions of a human figure?
    a) The Venus of Willendorf
    b) The Rosetta Stone
    c) The Bust of Nefertiti
    d) The Lascaux Bison

11. Which of the following metals was used before the Bronze Age, in the so-called "Chalcolithic" period?
    a) Silver
    b) Copper
    c) Iron
    d) Zinc

12. What makes the site of Çatalhöyük unique among Neolithic settlements?
    a) Its people built pyramids
    b) Homes were entered through the roof
    c) It had a complex sewage system
    d) It was surrounded by a large defensive wall

13. What ancient technique did humans use to create sharper stone tools during the Upper Paleolithic period?
    a) Metal casting
    b) Pressure flaking
    c) Sand polishing
    d) Hydraulic carving

14. What was a significant consequence of the development of pottery in early human societies?
    a) It allowed for better food storage and cooking
    b) It led to an increase in warfare
    c) It reduced the need for hunting
    d) It replaced stone tools

15. True or False: Humans stopped using stone tools entirely after the Bronze Age began.

ANSWERS

1. **c) Oldowan** – The Oldowan tool tradition (discovered in Africa) is the earliest known stone tool technology, dating back about 2.6 million years.

2. **d) Stone** – The earliest tools were made from chipped stone, which early hominins used for cutting, scraping, and pounding.

3. **b) Spain** – The oldest known cave paintings, found in Maltravieso Cave, Spain, are at least 64,000 years old.

4. **c) Neanderthals** – Recent dating of cave art in Spain (over 64,000 years ago) predates the known arrival of modern humans in Europe, suggesting Neanderthals were the artists—a revolutionary discovery.

5. **b) The Copper Age** – The Copper Age (Chalcolithic) preceded the Bronze Age, with copper tools used as early as 5,000 BCE.

6. **b) The development of agriculture** – The Neolithic period saw the rise of farming, which led to permanent settlements.

7. **b) Qafzeh Cave, Israel** – This site holds some of the oldest evidence of deliberate human burial (ca. 100,000 years ago), including a young individual buried with a red ochre pigment—implying ritual significance.

8. **a) Bone flute** – The oldest known musical instrument, a flute carved from a vulture bone, dates back over 50,000 years.

9. **a) To protect against the cold during Ice Age periods** – Sewing and tailored clothing became essential as humans migrated to colder regions.

10. **a) The Venus of Willendorf** – This small limestone figurine, dating to about 28,000 BCE, represents one of the earliest known depictions of a human figure.

11. **b) Copper** – The Chalcolithic (Copper Age) preceded the Bronze Age in many regions. Copper tools were used, but because copper is soft, its utility was limited until alloyed into bronze.

12. **b) Homes were entered through the roof** – At Çatalhöyük (~7500 BCE), homes were packed tightly with no streets, and people entered through ladders in the roof. This unusual design might have helped with defense and insulation.

13. **b) Pressure flaking** – This technique, used by Upper Paleolithic humans, involved pressing a tool against stone to create precise, sharp edges.

14. **a) It allowed for better food storage and cooking** – Pottery made it easier to store and transport food, supporting larger populations.

15. **False** – Although metal tools became dominant, stone tools were still used for many tasks, even into historical periods.

The Origins of Language

Language is one of the greatest achievements of human civilization. Without it, history as we know it wouldn't exist. But when did humans start speaking? What were the first writing systems? And what ancient scripts remain a mystery?

1. What is the leading theory about when spoken language first emerged?
   a) 30,000 years ago
   b) 3,000 years ago
   c) 100,000 years ago
   d) 1 million years ago

2. Which ancient writing system is the oldest known to historians?
   a) Egyptian hieroglyphs
   b) Sumerian cuneiform
   c) Chinese script
   d) Linear A

3. The Rosetta Stone was the key to deciphering which ancient language?
   a) Akkadian
   b) Mayan
   c) Egyptian hieroglyphs
   d) Etruscan

4. What feature made Sumerian cuneiform adaptable to other early languages like Akkadian, Hittite, and Elamite?
   a) It was phonetic and modular
   b) It had only 10 symbols
   c) It was an alphabetic script
   d) It used colors and textures instead of symbols

5. What is the earliest known example of written law?
   a) The Code of Ur-Nammu
   b) The Ten Commandments
   c) The Magna Carta
   d) The Twelve Tables

6. What is the oldest known undeciphered script?
   a) Rongorongo
   b) Linear A
   c) Meroitic script
   d) Indus Valley script

7. Which ancient civilization used oracle bones as a medium for some of the earliest known forms of writing in East Asia?
   a) The Babylonians
   b) The Egyptians
   c) The Shang Dynasty
   d) The Greeks

8. Which ancient script influenced the creation of the first alphabetic writing system, and by extension, Latin?
   a) Coptic
   b) Hieratic
   c) Phoenician
   d) Ugaritic

9. What ancient writing medium did Egyptians use to record information?
   a) Clay tablets
   b) Stone slabs
   c) Papyrus
   d) Wooden scrolls

10. What is the earliest known written story?
    a) The Odyssey
    b) The Epic of Gilgamesh
    c) The Iliad
    d) The Book of the Dead

11. Which civilization's script contained more than 1,000 different symbols?
    a) The Chinese
    b) The Egyptians
    c) The Sumerians
    d) The Minoans

12. Which of these reasons is *not* a reason for ancient languages to disappear?
    a) Natural disasters
    b) The invention of the printing press
    c) Invasions and cultural shifts
    d) The development of new alphabets

13. What linguistic mystery remains about the Basque language?
    a) It has no known relatives
    b) It was invented in the 19th century
    c) It was spoken on every continent
    d) It contains no verbs

14. What type of writing predated alphabets?
    a) Hieroglyphs
    b) Pictographs
    c) Cursive script
    d) Greek lettering

15. In what way did Hieratic script differ from traditional hieroglyphics in ancient Egypt?
    a) It was used only for tomb walls
    b) It was cursive and written with ink
    c) It had no religious significance
    d) It included numbers but no letters

ANSWERS

1. **c) 100,000 years ago** – While no one knows the exact date, most linguists believe spoken language emerged at least 70, 000 to 150,000 years ago, likely alongside Homo sapiens.

2. **b) Sumerian cuneiform** – The Sumerians, in Mesopotamia, created cuneiform writing around 3100 BCE, making it the oldest known writing system.

3. **c) Egyptian hieroglyphs** – The Rosetta Stone, discovered in 1799, contained the same text in three scripts (hieroglyphic, demotic, and Greek), helping scholars decipher Egyptian writing.

4. **a) It was phonetic and modular** – Cuneiform signs could represent sounds, syllables, or whole words, making it flexible enough to be adapted by multiple ancient cultures with different languages

5. **a) The Code of Ur-Nammu** – The Code of Ur-Nammu (c. 2100–2050 BCE) is the oldest extant law code in the world, predating Hammurabi (which is more famous and complete) by several centuries.

6. **d) Indus Valley script** – Also known as the Harappan script, it dates to c. 3500–1900 BCE. It has over 400 unique symbols, but no bilingual texts have been found to help decipher it.

7. **c) The Shang Dynasty** – They used oracle bones inscribed with early Chinese characters for divination and record-keeping.

8. **c) Phoenician** – The Phoenician script (c. 1050 BCE) was the first known alphabet, consisting only of consonants. It was adopted and adapted by the Greeks, who added vowels, forming the basis of many later alphabets.

9. **c) Papyrus** – Egyptians wrote on papyrus, an early form of paper made from reeds. This lightweight material revolutionized record-keeping.

10. **b) The Epic of Gilgamesh** – Dating to c. 2100 BCE, this Mesopotamian story is the oldest known literary work, describing the adventures of King Gilgamesh.

11. **b) The Egyptians** – Hieroglyphic writing contained over 1,000 symbols, making it complex to read and write.

12. **b) The invention of the printing press** – Rather than causing extinction, the printing press actually helped preserve and spread many languages.

13. **a) It has no known relatives** – Basque is an isolated language, meaning it is unrelated to any other known language.

14. **b) Pictographs** – The earliest writing began as pictographs (simple drawings representing objects) before evolving into symbols and alphabets.

15. **b) It was cursive and written with ink on papyrus** – Hieratic was a more fluid, simplified form of hieroglyphics used for everyday writing and administration. It was used by scribes on papyrus, much like cursive handwriting.

Megalithic Traces

Scattered across the world are enigmatic megalithic structures, some dating back thousands of years before the Pyramids. These colossal monuments leave us with more questions than answers. Who built them? How did they transport such massive stones? And what were they used for?

1. Göbekli Tepe, one of the world's oldest known temple sites, is located in which modern-day country?
   a) Turkey
   b) Egypt
   c) Greece
   d) Iran

2. What is the estimated age of Göbekli Tepe?
   a) 5,000 years old
   b) 7,000 years old
   c) 9,500 years old
   d) 12,000 years old

3. The Carnac stones, a vast collection of standing stones, are found in which country?
   a) France
   b) England
   c) Spain
   d) Ireland

4. What famous megalithic site aligns with the winter solstice, allowing the sun to shine directly into its central chamber?
   a) Stonehenge
   b) Newgrange
   c) Machu Picchu
   d) The Great Pyramid of Giza

5. True or False: Stonehenge was built all at once.

6. Which of the following is not typically considered a megalithic structure?
   a) Dolmen
   b) Menhir
   c) Ziggurat
   d) Stone circle

7. The Ba'albek stones in Lebanon include some of the largest cut stones in history. What is the weight of the largest stone, the "Stone of the Pregnant Woman"?
   a) 50 tons
   b) 200 tons
   c) 500 tons
   d) 1,000 tons

8. Which region has one of the highest densities of megalithic structures in the world?
   a) Central Asia
   b) Scandinavia
   c) Western Europe
   d) Northern Africa

9. What is a dolmen?
   a) A burial structure with large upright stones and a capstone
   b) A ceremonial temple complex
   c) A type of stone carving
   d) A natural rock formation mistaken for a human structure

10. What is unusual about the layout of the Callanish Stones in Scotland?
    a) They form the shape of a human figure when viewed from above
    b) They align with both lunar and solar events
    c) They were buried under a lake for centuries
    d) Each stone is inscribed with ogham script

11. Which megalithic site includes the largest known single stone moved by prehistoric people, weighing an estimated 280 tons?
    a) Stonehenge
    b) Baalbek, Lebanon
    c) Nata Playa, Egypt
    d) Durrington Walls, England

12. What sets Nabta Playa apart as a megalithic site?
    a) It includes the oldest known stone circle, predating Stonehenge
    b) It is built entirely out of granite
    c) It was carved into the side of a mountain
    d) It contains written proto-hieroglyphs

13. What is unique about the Tiahuanaco ruins in Bolivia?
    a) The stones seem to be cut with laser-like precision
    b) They were built underwater
    c) They contain inscriptions in an unknown language
    d) They were built by a civilization with no written records

14. What modern technology has helped reveal previously unknown megalithic sites?
    a) Sonar
    b) Lidar
    c) Radiocarbon dating
    d) Drones

15. What ancient civilization built the mysterious moai statues of Easter Island?
    a) The Aztecs
    b) The Rapa Nui
    c) The Mayans
    d) The Maori

ANSWERS

1. **a) Turkey** – Göbekli Tepe is in southeastern Turkey and is considered the oldest known temple complex.

2. **d) 12,000 years old** – Dating back to 9600 BCE, Göbekli Tepe was built by pre-agricultural hunter-gatherers, challenging the idea that civilizations needed farming to build monuments.

3. **a) France** – The Carnac stones in Brittany, France, consist of over 3,000 standing stones arranged in rows. Their purpose remains unknown.

4. **b) Newgrange** – Built around 3200 BCE in Ireland, Newgrange is older than Stonehenge and the Great Pyramid, and it aligns perfectly with the winter solstice.

5. **False** – Stonehenge was built in stages over 1,500 years, beginning around 3000 BCE.

6. **c) Ziggurat** – Ziggurats are stepped structures from ancient Mesopotamia and not part of the European megalithic tradition. The others—dolmens, menhirs, and stone circles—are classic megalithic forms.

7. **d) 1,000 tons** – The Stone of the Pregnant Woman in Ba'albek, Lebanon, is one of the largest cut stones in human history. It is estimated to weigh at least 1,000 tons, possibly as much as 1,650 tons.

8. **c) Western Europe** – Regions like Brittany (France), the British Isles, and the Iberian Peninsula are dense with megalithic sites, suggesting widespread shared practices or beliefs in the Neolithic and Chalcolithic periods.

9. **a) A burial structure with large upright stones and a capstone** – Dolmens are ancient stone tombs found across Europe, Asia, and Africa.

10. **b) They align with both lunar and solar events** – The Callanish Stones (c. 3000 BCE) are thought to track an 18.6-year lunar cycle, as well as solar positions. Their layout also suggests ritual or ceremonial use aligned with the heavens.

11. **b) Baalbek, Lebanon** – The "Stone of the Pregnant Woman" at Baalbek weighs over 280 tons and was never fully moved into position. Its scale dwarfs anything at Stonehenge and reflects remarkable prehistoric engineering.

12. **a) It includes the oldest known stone circle, predating Stonehenge** – Located in southern Egypt, Nabta Playa's stone circle may date to around 6000 BCE. It's considered the world's oldest known astronomical alignment, likely used by early pastoralists.

13. **a) The stones seem to be cut with laser-like precision** – The Tiahuanaco ruins in Bolivia feature interlocking stones so precisely carved that some researchers believe they may have used advanced techniques.

14. **b) Lidar** – Lidar (Light Detection and Ranging) is helping archaeologists discover hidden megalithic structures buried under dense vegetation.

15. **b) The Rapa Nui** – The Rapa Nui people of Easter Island carved and transported the moai statues, some of which weigh over 80 tons.

The Birth of Agriculture and Civilization

The shift from hunter-gatherer societies to settled farming communities was one of the most revolutionary changes in human history. It led to permanent settlements, cities, writing, and civilization itself. But how much do you really know about this crucial turning point?

1. The first known domesticated crops were cultivated in which region?
   a) The Amazon Rainforest
   b) The Middle East
   c) Europe
   d) Southern Africa

2. Which grain is often considered a foundation of early agriculture?
   a) Barley
   b) Maize
   c) Rice
   d) Quinoa

3. True or False: The transition to farming happened suddenly, over just a few generations.

4. What major lifestyle change did agriculture bring about?
   a) Nomadic tribes increased in number
   b) Societies became more hierarchical
   c) People lived shorter lives
   d) People stopped eating meat

5. What was one of the first domesticated animals in early agricultural societies?
   a) Chicken
   b) Sheep
   c) Pig
   d) Dog

6. What early civilization was known for its advanced urban planning, with straight streets and complex drainage systems?
   a) The Sumerians
   b) The Indus Valley Civilization
   c) The Hittites
   d) The Mycenaeans

7. Mesopotamia, often called the "Cradle of Civilization," was located between which two rivers?
   a) The Ganges and Yamuna
   b) The Nile and the Jordan
   c) The Tigris and Euphrates
   d) The Yellow and Yangtze

8. What innovation helped early farmers transition from foraging to planned agriculture?
   a) Iron ploughs
   b) Pottery for seed storage
   c) Domesticated horses
   d) Wheeled carts

9. Which of these is *not* a reason the Indus Valley Civilization is considered a mystery?
   a) Their script remains undeciphered
   b) No temples or palaces have been found
   c) The civilization vanished without a clear explanation
   d) Their cities were built entirely underground

10. The Yellow River is known as the birthplace of civilization in which modern country?
    a) India
    b) China
    c) Japan
    d) Vietnam

11. Which early farming society cultivated maize (corn)?
    a) The Maya
    b) The Egyptians
    c) The Celts
    d) The Persians

12. True or False: Early farming societies were more egalitarian than hunter-gatherer groups.

13. Which ancient city, founded around 4000 BCE, is believed to be the first true city-state with defined political structures?
    a) Babylon
    b) Eridu
    c) Uruk
    d) Thebes

14. What early farming tool revolutionized agriculture, allowing for more efficient planting?
    a) The sickle
    b) The plow
    c) The wheel
    d) The hoe

15. What civilization built the oldest known city, Jericho?
    a) The Sumerians
    b) The Natufians
    c) The Phoenicians
    d) The Babylonians

ANSWERS

1. **b) The Middle East** – The region named The Fertile Crescent, which includes parts of modern-day Iraq, Syria, Israel, and Turkey, was home to the first domesticated crops like wheat and barley, around 10,000 BCE.

2. **a) Barley** – One of the earliest domesticated grains, barley was a staple in Mesopotamia and Egypt and was often used for making bread and beer.

3. **False** – The shift to farming took thousands of years and occurred in different regions at different times.

4. **b) Societies became more hierarchical** – Agriculture led to surpluses, which allowed some people to specialize in other tasks, creating social classes and ruling elites.

5. **d) Dog** – Dogs were domesticated from wolves likely before the advent of agriculture, around 15,000–20,000 years ago. They played roles in protection, hunting, and possibly even herding in early societies.

6. **b) The Indus Valley Civilization** – Cities like Harappa and Mohenjo-Daro had grid-like streets, multi-story houses, and advanced drainage systems, built around 2600 BCE.

7. **c) The Tigris and Euphrates** – Mesopotamia (modern-day Iraq and parts of Syria) developed complex societies, writing, and the first cities.

8. **b) Pottery for seed storage** – Pottery allowed for long-term seed storage, which made planned sowing possible. It also enabled food surplus and preservation, key to the shift from seasonal foraging to sedentary farming.

9. **d) Their cities were built entirely underground** – They were above-ground, highly organized cities, famous for their brick architecture and street grids, not subterranean design.

10. **b) China** – The Yellow River was home to some of China's first agricultural communities, such as the Yangshao and Longshan cultures.

11. **a) The Maya** – Corn was domesticated in Mesoamerica around 7,000 years ago and became the foundation of Mayan, Aztec, and Inca agriculture.

12. **False** – Many early farming societies became more unequal, as landowners and rulers controlled food surpluses. Hunter-gatherers often had more equality and better diets!

13. **c) Uruk** – Uruk, in southern Mesopotamia, was likely the first true city-state, with around 40,000 people at its height. It had monumental architecture, a bureaucracy, and possibly even kingship.

14. **b) The plow** – Invented in Mesopotamia, the plow increased food production, allowing societies to grow larger.

15. **b) The Natufians** – The Natufians (around 10,000 BCE) built Jericho, one of the earliest known settlements, with walls and circular stone houses.

Final Score: How Did You Do?

- **60–75 correct: Master of the Ages!** Your knowledge of early human history is legendary.
- **45–59 correct: Prehistoric Prodigy** – You know your flint from your fire!
- **30–44 correct: Promising Time Traveler** – You've got the basics down but might struggle in the prehistoric wild.
- **15–29 correct: Stone Age Struggler** – You're getting there, but you might need a few more lifetimes to master prehistory.
- **0–14 correct: Lost in the Past** – Looks like you need a time machine to catch up!

THE LOST KINGDOMS OF ANTIQUITY

Before there were maps of Africa neatly drawn with modern borders, there were mighty kingdoms whose power stretched across deserts, rainforests, and river valleys—their wealth dazzling, their cities legendary, and their stories often hidden beneath the sands of time. This chapter whisks you away to the bustling markets of Timbuktu, the gold-laden caravans of Mali, the soaring stone towers of Great Zimbabwe, and the monumental pyramids of Kush. These weren't mere footnotes in history; they were thriving, sophisticated civilizations, complete with fierce queens, fearless traders, master builders, and scholars whose wisdom lit up the ancient world. From the astounding legacy of Mansa Musa to the ingenious irrigation of the Garamantes, the lost kingdoms of Africa were forces to be reckoned with—long before European explorers even set sail.

Yet, as with many great tales of antiquity, these stories come wrapped in layers of mystery. How did the Kingdom of Ghana amass such staggering fortunes? And why do the astonishing stone ruins of Great Zimbabwe continue to puzzle historians today?

Did you know...?

Ancient Egyptians believed the heart, not the brain, was the seat of thought, emotion, and memory. During mummification, they carefully preserved the heart for the afterlife but often threw away the brain, removing it through the nose with hooks. This practice lasted for centuries, despite the brain being the actual control center. Their spiritual logic outweighed anatomical accuracy—until much later science proved otherwise.

The Rise and Fall of African Powers

Africa was home to some of the most powerful and influential empires in history, yet many remain overlooked in mainstream historical narratives. From the wealth of Mali to the mysteries of Great Zimbabwe, these civilizations left lasting legacies.

1. The Aksumite Empire was one of the first major African civilizations to adopt which religion?
   a) Islam
   b) Christianity
   c) Judaism
   d) Zoroastrianism

2. Mansa Musa, the ruler of Mali, is often considered:
   a) The wealthiest person in history
   b) A legendary warrior king
   c) The founder of Timbuktu
   d) The first Muslim ruler of Africa

3. The Kushite Kingdom ruled over which famous civilization for nearly a century?
   a) The Roman Empire
   b) Ancient Egypt
   c) Carthage
   d) The Greek city-states

4. True or False: Great Zimbabwe was built by ancient Egyptians.

5. What was the city of Timbuktu *not* famous for during the Mali Empire:
   a) Its advanced naval fleet that patrolled the Niger River
   b) Vast trading networks
   c) Centers of learning and scholarship
   d) Gold Mines

6. Which ancient African kingdom was famous for its ironworking technology and is one of the earliest known in sub-Saharan Africa?
a) Nok
b) Axum
c) Mali
d) Kush

7. Which empire built the Lalibela rock-hewn churches, considered an architectural wonder?
a) Zagwe Dynasty
b) Mali
c) Kush
d) Great Zimbabwe

8. The Kingdom of Ghana (not the modern country) was known for controlling trade in:
a) Spices
b) Gold and salt
c) Iron and copper
d) Silk and ivory

9. Which of these is *not* a reason that Aksum declined as a major empire?
a) Drought and environmental changes
b) Invasions by Islamic forces
c) A ban on written communication
d) Decline in trade routes

10. The rulers of the Kushite Kingdom were unique because:
a) They were often female
b) They built pyramids like the Egyptians
c) They wrote in the Meroitic script, which remains undeciphered
d) They invented the decimal system

11. Carthage, Rome's great rival, was founded by which ancient civilization?
    a) The Greeks
    b) The Phoenicians
    c) The Persians
    d) The Egyptians

12. What was a unique architectural feature of the Great Zimbabwe civilization?
    a) Step pyramids
    b) Rock-cut churches
    c) Massive stone enclosures without mortar
    d) Adobe palaces with gold-plated roofs

13. What ancient African region is thought to have been a key player in Red Sea trade and is sometimes linked to the biblical Land of Punt?
    a) Nubia
    b) Axum
    c) Garamantes
    d) Great Zimbabwe

14. What ancient African civilization was described by the Romans as the "land of the Garamantes"?
    a) Aksum
    b) Mali
    c) Carthage
    d) A desert kingdom In Libya

15. The Sudanese pyramids at Meroë were built by which African civilization?
    a) Mali
    b) Kush
    c) Aksum
    d) Carthage

ANSWERS

1. **b) Christianity** – The Aksumite Empire (modern-day Ethiopia and Eritrea) became one of the earliest Christian states in the 4th century CE, long before most of Europe.

2. **a) The wealthiest person in history** – Mansa Musa (r. 1312–1337) controlled gold-rich Mali, and his lavish spending during his pilgrimage to Mecca caused inflation in Egypt for years.

3. **b) Ancient Egypt** – The Kushites ruled as the 25th Dynasty of Egypt from 747–656 BCE, sometimes called the "Black Pharaohs."

4. **False** – Great Zimbabwe (11th–15th century CE) was built by the Shona people, not outsiders. European explorers once falsely claimed it must have been built by foreign civilizations.

5. **a) Its advanced naval fleet that patrolled the Niger River** – While Timbuktu was located near the Niger River, it was not known for a military or naval presence — trade and scholarship were its true strengths.

6. **a) Nok** – The Nok culture of present-day Nigeria dates back to around 1000 BCE. It is renowned for its advanced iron smelting and distinctive terracotta sculptures—some of the oldest in Africa.

7. **a) Zagwe Dynasty** – The stunning rock-hewn churches of Lalibela (12th–13th century) were carved into solid rock, a UNESCO World Heritage Site.

8. **b) Gold and salt** – The Ghana Empire (not the modern country) controlled lucrative trade routes, connecting West Africa to the Mediterranean world.

9. **c) A ban on written communication** – Aksum was known for its inscriptions and early adoption of writing systems.

10. **d) They invented the decimal system** – The decimal system has roots in ancient India and Mesopotamia, not in Kushite innovation.

11. **b) The Phoenicians** – Carthage was a Phoenician colony, founded around 814 BCE in modern Tunisia.

12. **c) Massive stone enclosures without mortar** – Great Zimbabwe (11th–15th centuries CE) featured sophisticated dry-stone architecture, including the Great Enclosure—the largest ancient structure in sub-Saharan Africa.

13. **b) Axum** – Axum was a maritime trading empire with connections across the Red Sea and Indian Ocean. Its wealth and exotic exports led some to associate it with the semi-mythical Land of Punt mentioned in Egyptian texts.

14. **d) A desert kingdom in Libya** – The Garamantes lived in the Saharan desert and created advanced irrigation systems.

15. **b) Kush** – The Kushites built pyramids at Meroë, which have steeper sides and outnumber Egyptian pyramids.

The Middle East – Masters of Metal and Builders of Empire

The Middle East was the cradle of civilization, home to powerful empires, mysterious kingdoms, and lost peoples. While names like Babylon and Persia are well known, others—like the Hittites, Elamites, and Mitanni—have remained in the shadows.

1. The Hittites were one of the first civilizations to master which game-changing technology?
   a) Bronze smelting
   b) Ironworking
   c) Chariot warfare
   d) Siege engines

2. The Battle of Kadesh (1274 BCE), between the Hittites and Egyptians, was significant because:
   a) It was the first recorded battle in history
   b) It resulted in the world's first known peace treaty
   c) It led to the fall of the Hittite Empire
   d) It was fought with Greek mercenaries

3. Which powerful Mesopotamian city was destroyed and salted by the Assyrians as a brutal warning to other cities?
   a) Babylon
   b) Nineveh
   c) Susa
   d) Elam

4. Which city is often credited with the birth of astronomy and celestial mapping, thanks to its priest-astronomers?
   a) Nineveh
   b) Babylon
   c) Ur
   d) Eridu

5. What surprising aspect of Sumerian medicine has been discovered through surviving texts?
   a) Use of iron surgical tools
   b) Awareness of antibiotics from mold
   c) Separation of magical and empirical healing practices
   d) Early vaccination techniques

6. In the biblical legend of the Ten Lost Tribes of Israel, it is *not* suggested they were:
   a) Exiled by the Assyrians and vanished
   b) Absorbed into other cultures
   c) Enslaved by the Babylonians
   d) The ancestors of various modern ethnic groups

7. Which of the following Mesopotamian innovations predates the use of coinage and served as a medium of standardized exchange?
   a) Clay tablets
   b) Grain tokens
   c) Weighed silver bars (shekels)
   d) Bead strings

8. What Indo-European deity names appear in the treaties of the ancient Mitanni Kingdom, suggesting foreign influence?
   a) Thor and Odin
   b) Indra and Varuna
   c) Zeus and Hermes
   d) Ra and Osiris

9. What are the Sea Peoples, a mysterious confederation of invaders, *not* thought to have contributed to:
   a) The founding of the Roman Republic
   b) The fall of the Hittites
   c) The collapse of multiple Bronze Age civilizations
   d) The rise of the Iron Age

10. What was significant about the city of Mari on the Euphrates?
    a) It was the first to use bronze tools
    b) It housed a vast archive of clay tablets offering insights into diplomacy
    c) It was an early Christian pilgrimage site
    d) It had the oldest known ziggurat

11. What was unique about the Hittite language compared to other ancient Middle Eastern tongues?
    a) It was the only known African language in Mesopotamia
    b) It was the first recorded Semitic language
    c) It was an Indo-European language, unlike neighboring civilizations
    d) It used an undeciphered pictographic script

12. Which of the following was a major religious innovation attributed to the Persian Achaemenid Empire?
    a) The worship of gods as animals
    b) The codification of temple rituals
    c) The promotion of monotheistic Zoroastrianism
    d) The first divine kingship ideology

13. Which civilization created the first known empire by uniting multiple city-states under one ruler around 2334 BCE?
    a) Hittites
    b) Akkadians
    c) Sumerians
    d) Elamites

14. In early Mesopotamian cosmology, the universe was believed to be structured as:
    a) A flat disk floating in water, with a dome sky
    b) A giant cube with rivers marking its edges
    c) A three-level pyramid representing heaven, earth, and underworld
    d) An eternal spiral with divine centers

15. The Kingdom of Urartu, a lesser-known ancient Middle Eastern state, is believed to be the ancestor of which modern-day nation?
    a) Iran
    b) Armenia
    c) Iraq
    d) Israel

ANSWERS

1. **b) Ironworking** – The Hittites were among the first to develop iron metallurgy, giving them a military edge over bronze-using civilizations.

2. **b) It resulted in the world's first known peace treaty** – The Treaty of Kadesh between Ramses II of Egypt and the Hittites is the oldest surviving peace treaty. A replica is even displayed at the United Nations headquarters.

3. **d) Elam** – The Elamite capital of **Susa** was destroyed by Assyrian king Ashurbanipal in 647 BCE. The city was razed, and salt was spread over the land—a symbolic act of total annihilation.

4. **b) Babylon** – Babylonian astronomers kept detailed star records and developed early forms of ephemerides and zodiac divisions. Their celestial observations informed both astrology and proto-scientific thinking.

5. **c) Separation of magical and empirical healing practices** – Some surviving medical texts distinguish between diagnosis-based prescriptions (e.g. herbal treatments, bandaging) and magical spells—showing an early awareness of medical cause and effect.

6. **c) Enslaved by the Babylonians** – While the Babylonians did exile the people of Judah (leading to the Babylonian Captivity), it was the Assyrians who conquered the northern kingdom of Israel and scattered the Ten Lost Tribes.

7. **c) Weighed silver bars (shekels)** – Before coins, the Mesopotamians used weighed silver (measured in shekels and talents) as a medium of exchange, especially in trade and contracts. This was a precursor to money.

8. **b) Indra and Varuna** – Unusually, Mitanni rulers invoked Hindu gods in treaties, suggesting ties to Indo-Aryan cultures.

9. **d) The founding of the Roman Republic** – The Sea Peoples, an enigmatic group who helped trigger the Bronze Age Collapse, wreaked havoc across the eastern Mediterranean, toppling cities and weakening empires, including the Hittites and Egyptians. Their activity predates the founding of Rome by several centuries, and they had no involvement in its establishment.

10. **b) It housed a vast archive of clay tablets offering insights into diplomacy** – Mari was a cultural and diplomatic hub. Over 20,000 clay tablets were uncovered, detailing trade, religion, and international relations with Egypt, Babylon, and beyond.

11. **c) It was an Indo-European language, unlike neighboring civilizations** – While surrounded by Semitic (Akkadian) and Sumerian speakers, the Hittites spoke an Indo-European language, distantly related to English and Latin.

12. **c) The promotion of monotheistic Zoroastrianism** – Zoroastrianism, promoted under Achaemenid rulers like Cyrus and Darius, was centered around the worship of Ahura Mazda and emphasized moral dualism—possibly influencing later Abrahamic religions.

13. **b) Akkadians** – Sargon of Akkad established the world's first known empire by conquering Sumerian city-states and forming a centralized state, spreading the Akkadian language and bureaucratic practices.

14. **a) A flat disk floating in water, with a dome sky** – Mesopotamians believed the earth was a flat disc surrounded by a cosmic ocean, with a solid dome overhead (the sky) where gods dwelled—a worldview echoed in other ancient cultures.

15. **b) Armenia** – The Kingdom of Urartu (9th–6th century BCE) occupied modern-day Armenia and eastern Turkey and is believed to be the predecessor of Armenian culture.

Secrets of the Americas

Before Europeans arrived, the Americas were home to vast, sophisticated civilizations, some of which mysteriously disappeared or were long overlooked. From the enigmatic collapse of the Maya to the lost cities of the Amazon, many questions remain unanswered.

1. What is one of the earliest known complex civilizations in Mesoamerica, often called the "mother culture" of later civilizations like the Maya and Aztec?
   a) Maya
   b) Olmec
   c) Toltec
   d) Zapotec

2. What is the name of the lost city in the Amazon that recent discoveries suggest was part of a massive, advanced civilization?
   a) El Dorado
   b) Ciudad Blanca
   c) Caral-Supe
   d) The Xingu Cities

3. Which civilization built the enormous city of Cahokia in what is now the United States?
   a) The Iroquois
   b) The Mississippians
   c) The Ancestral Puebloans
   d) The Olmecs

4. True or False: The Comanche Empire was one of the most powerful Native American forces in history, controlling vast territories and resisting European colonization.

5. The Mayans are famous for their Long Count Calendar, which led to doomsday predictions in what year?
   a) 1492
   b) 1776
   c) 2012
   d) 2020

6. The Nazca Lines, massive geoglyphs carved into the desert, are located in which modern-day country?
   a) Mexico
   b) Peru
   c) Bolivia
   d) Chile

7. Which civilization created the first known writing system in the Americas?
   a) The Inca
   b) The Olmecs
   c) The Maya
   d) The Chavín

8. The Olmec heads—some weighing over 20 tons—are believed to represent what?
   a) Their gods
   b) Rulers or ballplayers
   c) Astronomical deities
   d) Warriors from rival tribes

9. The Tupi-Guarani people of South America are believed to have influenced which modern country's culture and language?
   a) Argentina
   b) Brazil
   c) Venezuela
   d) Peru

10. The Chavín civilization, one of the earliest known cultures of the Andes, was famous for:
    a) Monumental stone heads
    b) Goldworking and mysterious art
    c) Step pyramids
    d) A vast road network

11. Which ancient South American civilization engineered an advanced system of subterranean aqueducts to bring water to dry regions?
    a) Moche
    b) Nazca
    c) Chavín
    d) Inca

12. The Moche civilization of Peru is famous for which distinctive artwork?
    a) Enormous stone heads
    b) Highly realistic pottery featuring people and animals
    c) Intricate feathered headdresses
    d) Giant stone pyramids

13. What was unique about the Inca Empire's communication system?
    a) They had the first postal service in the world
    b) They used knotted cords called quipu instead of writing
    c) They created the first alphabet in the Americas
    d) They trained parrots to carry messages

14. Which Mesoamerican civilization dominated central Mexico before the rise of the Aztecs and built the massive pyramids at Teotihuacan?
    a) The Toltecs
    b) The Mixtecs
    c) The Zapotecs
    d) The Teotihuacanos

15. The Wari and Tiwanaku civilizations are known for what urban and cultural innovation, later adopted by the Inca?
a) Step pyramids
b) Raised-field agriculture and road networks
c) Domed observatories
d) Glass mosaic palaces

ANSWERS

1. **b) Olmec** – Flourishing from around 1500–400 BCE, the **Olmec** created monumental art (including colossal heads), developed early writing and calendars, and laid the cultural groundwork for later civilizations like the Maya.

2. **d) The Xingu Cities** – Recent discoveries using LiDAR technology have revealed vast urban networks in the Amazon, suggesting that complex civilizations once flourished there before being overtaken by the jungle.

3. **b) The Mississippians** – Cahokia (600–1400 CE) was the largest pre-Columbian city in North America, with mounds, plazas, and an advanced trade network. Its decline is still a mystery.

4. **True** – The Comanche Empire (1700s–1800s) was a dominant military force that controlled vast lands in Texas and the Great Plains. They were feared warriors and expert horse riders.

5. **c) 2012** – The Maya Long Count Calendar ended a cycle in 2012, sparking apocalyptic predictions—but it was simply the start of a new cycle, not the end of the world.

6. **b) Peru** – The Nazca Lines (500 BCE–500 CE) are enormous geoglyphs of animals, geometric shapes, and figures, only fully visible from the sky.

7. **b) The Olmecs** – The Olmecs (1500–400 BCE) developed the earliest writing system in Mesoamerica, which influenced the Maya script.

8. **b) Rulers or ballplayers** – The Olmec colossal heads are widely believed to depict rulers or elite ballplayers. Their individualized facial features suggest they represent specific people, and some were found near ball courts.

9. **b) Brazil** – The Tupi-Guarani heavily influenced Brazilian culture, and many Portuguese words come from their language.

10. **b) Goldworking and mysterious art** – The Chavín civilization (900–200 BCE) was known for intricate goldwork, stone carvings, and eerie feline-inspired artwork.

11. **b) Nazca** – The Nazca engineered puquios, underground aqueducts with spiral access points. These systems provided water year-round in an otherwise arid environment, demonstrating advanced hydrological knowledge.

12. **b) Highly realistic pottery featuring people and animals** – The Moche civilization (100–800 CE) created stunningly detailed ceramics, depicting everyday life, gods, and even medical procedures.

13. **b) They used knotted cords called quipu instead of writing** – The Inca had no written script but used quipu (knotted cords) to record information and manage their empire.

14. **d) The Teotihuacanos** – The builders of Teotihuacan (100 BCE–550 CE), with its enormous Pyramids of the Sun and Moon, remain mysterious, as they left no written records.

15. **b) Raised-field agriculture and road networks** – Both Wari and Tiwanaku developed raised-field farming and road systems that enabled imperial expansion. The Inca later refined these models, building thousands of miles of roads and terraced agriculture.

The First European Civilizations

Before the rise of Classical Greece and Rome, sophisticated cultures flourished across Europe. From the Minoans and Mycenaeans to the mysterious Tartessos, these societies left behind ruins, legends, and unsolved mysteries.

1. The Minoan civilization flourished on which Mediterranean island?
   a) Cyprus
   b) Crete
   c) Sardinia
   d) Sicily

2. What legendary creature is associated with the Labyrinth at Knossos in Greece?
   a) The Hydra
   b) The Minotaur
   c) The Chimera
   d) The Basilisk

3. The Minoan civilization mysteriously declined around 1450 BCE. What is one leading theory for its collapse?
   a) A devastating earthquake and tsunami
   b) A Persian invasion
   c) A plague
   d) A slave uprising

4. The Mycenaeans, Greece's first great civilization, are best known for their connection to which epic tale?
   a) The Aeneid
   b) The Iliad
   c) The Argonautica
   d) The Odyssey

5. Which ancient European people were described by Greek writers as being matrilineal and possibly practiced female-led governance?
   a) Scythians
   b) Thracians
   c) Picts
   d) Lemnians

6. True or False: The city of Troy, famously besieged in the Trojan War, was a purely mythical place.

7. The Tartessians were an advanced, wealthy civilization located in which modern-day country?
   a) Italy
   b) France
   c) Spain
   d) Greece

8. Which Iron Age Celtic tribe in Gaul built a massive fortified city called Bibracte, and later allied with Julius Caesar before turning against him?
   a) Helvetii
   b) Aedui
   c) Arverni
   d) Sequani

9. Which lost European civilization may have inspired legends of Atlantis?
   a) The Mycenaeans
   b) The Minoans
   c) The Etruscans
   d) The Celts

10. The Lepenski Vir settlement in modern-day Serbia is notable for which cultural innovation around 7000 BCE?
    a) Domestication of horses
    b) Monumental stone fish sculptures
    c) Use of copper weapons
    d) Large-scale wheat cultivation

11. The Etruscan language remains a mystery because:
    a) It has never been discovered
    b) It is not Indo-European and has few surviving texts
    c) It was only spoken, never written
    d) No one knows where the Etruscans lived

12. Which ancient European culture built megalithic tombs and stone circles before written history?
    a) The Picts
    b) The Bell Beaker Culture
    c) The Scythians
    d) The Thracians

13. The Celts once dominated much of Europe. What happened to them?
    a) They vanished without a trace
    b) They were absorbed or conquered by Rome and later nations
    c) They migrated to North Africa
    d) They were wiped out by the introduction of diseases from the Americas

14. The Vinca culture (c. 5000 BCE), one of Europe's oldest societies, had what advanced feature?
    a) A writing system
    b) Large pyramids
    c) Domesticated horses
    d) Glass-making

15. True or False: The legendary city of Tartessos has never been definitively found.

ANSWERS

1. **b) Crete** – The Minoan civilization (c. 3000–1450 BCE) was centered on Crete and is considered Europe's first advanced society, famous for its elaborate palaces, art, and trade networks.

2. **b) The Minotaur** – According to Greek mythology, the Labyrinth of Knossos housed the half-man, half-bull Minotaur, which was eventually slain by Theseus.

3. **a) A devastating earthquake and tsunami** – One leading theory suggests that the eruption of Thera (modern Santorini) around 1600 BCE triggered a tsunami that weakened the Minoans, leading to their conquest by the Mycenaeans.

4. **b) The Iliad** – The Mycenaeans (1600–1100 BCE) were the inspiration for Homer's Iliad, which tells of the Trojan War and the siege of Troy.

5. **c) Picts** - Early accounts of the Picts in Scotland suggest matrilineal descent, though this remains debated. Some sources claim that kingship passed through the female line, possibly indicating matrilineal governance.

6. **False** – The city of Troy was real! Archaeologists have found the ruins of a city in modern Turkey that aligns with Homer's descriptions.

7. **b) Aedui** – The Aedui were initially Roman allies but later became involved in the Gallic resistance led by Vercingetorix. Their city of Bibracte was a major political and economic center in Iron Age Gaul.

8. **a) Silver** – Tartessos was famous for its rich silver mines, which attracted traders from the Mediterranean.

9. **b) The Minoans** – Some scholars believe that the story of Atlantis may have been inspired by the destruction of the Minoan civilization, particularly after the Thera eruption.

10. **b) Monumental stone fish sculptures** – Lepenski Vir is one of the earliest sedentary settlements in Europe and is famous for its stylized stone fish-human **sculptures**—suggesting an early symbolic or religious system linked to river life.

11. **b) It is not Indo-European and has few surviving texts** – Unlike Latin or Greek, Etruscan is unrelated to most known languages, making it difficult to decipher. The Etruscan culture heavily influenced the later Roman culture.

12. **b) The Bell Beaker Culture** – This prehistoric European society (c. 2800–1800 BCE) built stone circles, tombs, and early metallurgy sites. However, earlier Neolithic peoples (e.g., builders of Stonehenge, Newgrange) were the primary creators of the oldest megalithic monuments.

13. **b) They were absorbed or conquered by Rome and later nations** – The Celts once dominated much of Western and Central Europe, but Rome conquered them, and Germanic and Slavic peoples replaced them in many areas.

14. **a) A writing system** – The Vinca culture (c. 5000 BCE) in the Balkans may have had one of the earliest known writing systems, though its symbols remain undeciphered.

15. **True** – Despite many theories, no one has definitively discovered Tartessos, making it one of Europe's greatest archaeological mysteries.

Roman Oddities

Think You Know Everything About Ancient Rome? Think Again! The Roman Empire is one of the most famous civilizations in history, but even seasoned history buffs might be surprised by some of its stranger secrets, from lost legions and mysterious ruins to hidden rival kingdoms.

1. The Ninth Legion mysteriously vanished in which part of the Roman Empire?
   a) Gaul
   b) Britannia
   c) Germania
   d) Parthia

2. True or False: The Romans reached China through trade and possible lost explorers.

3. What was the name of the legendary kingdom that never fell to Rome, despite multiple invasions?
   a) Armenia
   b) Dacia
   c) Nabataea
   d) Parthia

4. Which future Roman emperor was famously captured by pirates as a young man and later demanded his own ransom be doubled?
   a) Julius Caesar
   b) Augustus
   c) Nero
   d) Claudius

5. Which Roman emperor famously tried to appoint his horse as a consul, shocking the Roman elite?
   a) Nero
   b) Caligula
   c) Commodus
   d) Claudius

6. What deadly weapon did the Romans refuse to use, despite their military genius?
   a) Poison gas
   b) Flaming arrows
   c) War elephants
   d) Biological warfare

7. The Limes Germanicus was a system of:
   a) Aqueducts
   b) Border fortifications
   c) Underground roads
   d) Secret Roman temples

8. The city of Petra, known for its rock-cut architecture, was part of which kingdom that coexisted with Rome?
   a) Dacia
   b) Nabataea
   c) Sarmatia
   d) Hibernia

9. Which country was *never* fully conquered by Rome?
   a) France
   b) Spain
   c) Scotland
   d) Turkey

10. Roman coins have been found in which unexpected location?
    a) Australia
    b) Japan
    c) Iceland
    d) South Africa

11. What language did the Romans encounter in Britain that was completely unrelated to Latin?
    a) Gaelic
    b) Basque
    c) Pictish
    d) Etruscan

12. The Romans once built a bridge across which major European river in just 10 days?
    a) The Danube
    b) The Rhine
    c) The Thames
    d) The Seine

13. True or False: A Roman Emperor was once captured in battle and used as a footstool by his enemies.

14. Which ancient empire defeated Rome and stole its battle standards, humiliating them?
    a) The Huns
    b) The Parthians
    c) The Egyptians
    d) The Scythians

15. The largest known surviving Roman mosaic was not found in Italy, but in which country?
    a) Turkey
    b) England
    c) Tunisia
    d) Jordan

ANSWERS

1. **b) Britannia** – The Legio IX Hispana was one of Rome's most elite legions, but it vanished from historical records in Britain around 120 CE. Some believe they were destroyed by the Picts, while others think they were sent elsewhere and lost in battle.

2. **True** – Roman records mention envoys reaching China's Han Dynasty around 166 CE, and some historians speculate that a lost group of Roman soldiers may have settled in China's Gansu province.

3. **d) Parthia** – Despite repeated wars, Parthia never fell to Rome. It dealt several crushing defeats to Roman armies, including the infamous Battle of Carrhae (53 BCE).

4. **a) Julius Caesar** – As a young man, Julius Caesar was kidnapped by Cilician pirates. He maintained his composure, insisted they raise his ransom, and later returned with a fleet to capture his captors.

5. **b) Caligula** – Emperor Caligula is said to have loved his horse Incitatus so much that he planned to make him a consul, highlighting both his eccentricity and the decadence of his reign.

6. **a) Poison gas** – Unlike some ancient civilizations, Rome never widely used poison gas or chemical warfare, despite its military innovations.

7. **b) Border fortifications** – The Limes Germanicus was a 1,500-kilometer network of walls and forts marking Rome's frontier in Germany.

8. **b) Nabataea** – Petra, famous for its rock-cut tombs and temples, was part of the Nabataean Kingdom, which Rome annexed in 106 CE.

9. **c) Scotland** – The Romans never fully conquered Scotland, despite multiple invasions. Instead, they built Hadrian's Wall to keep out the fierce Caledonian tribes.

10. **c) Iceland** – Roman coins have been found in Iceland, possibly brought there by Viking traders who encountered Roman currency in Europe.

11. **c) Pictish** – The Picts of Scotland spoke a now-lost language, likely unrelated to Latin or Gaelic.

12. **b) The Rhine** – In 55 BCE, Julius Caesar ordered his legions to build a bridge across the Rhine River in just 10 days, allowing them to invade Germania.

13. **True** – Emperor Valerian was captured by the Persian king Shapur I in 260 CE. According to legend, he was used as a footstool before dying in captivity.

14. **b) The Parthians** – At the Battle of Carrhae, the Parthians annihilated a Roman army and captured their battle standards, a devastating humiliation.

15. **c) Tunisia** – The largest Roman mosaic ever discovered was unearthed in Tunisia, part of Rome's African provinces.

Final Score: How Did You Do?

- 60–75 correct: Historical Hero
- 45–59 correct: Seasoned Scholar
- 30–44 correct: Time-Travel Trainee
- 15–29 correct: Trivia Tourist
- 0–14 correct: Chronologically Confused

MEDIEVAL AND RENAISSANCE ENIGMAS

THE DARK AGES – MYTHS, LEGENDS AND UNKNOWN HEROES

When the Roman Empire fell, the world didn't fall silent—it roared with new voices, new powers, and new legends. This chapter takes you into that misunderstood era where history meets myth, and where tales of shadowy warlords, fearless explorers, and unexpected thinkers shaped the future of continents. Castles rose from ruins, seafarers pushed the edges of the known world, and brave chroniclers wrote the first lines of stories that would echo through the centuries. Far from being a time of darkness, this age was alive with ambition and survival, as old worlds crumbled and new ones began to rise.

Prepare to unravel the mysteries of an era filled with twists and turns. What happened after the emperors laid down their crowns? Who kept knowledge alive in the face of chaos? And what secrets still linger in the sagas and ruins of this enigmatic time?

Did you know...?

During the early medieval period, Irish monks were among the most prolific preservers of ancient knowledge. As much of Europe was fragmented by war and instability, isolated Irish monasteries copied classical texts by hand—sometimes adding whimsical doodles and jokes in the margins. Without them, many works of Greek and Roman philosophy, science, and literature might have been lost forever. Their quiet scribbling helped spark Europe's later intellectual revival.

The Aftermath of Rome

The fall of the Western Roman Empire reshaped Europe's political and cultural landscape, birthing new kingdoms, traditions, and conflicts. From the rise of Germanic rulers and Byzantine resilience to the preservation of Roman ideals, this era laid the foundations for medieval Europe's complex identity.

1. In what year did the Western Roman Empire officially fall?
   a) 410 AD
   b) 476 AD
   c) 533 AD
   d) 1453 AD

2. Who was the last de facto emperor of the Western Roman Empire?
   a) Julius Nepos
   b) Romulus Augustulus
   c) Honorius
   d) Theodosius I

3. Which Germanic leader deposed the last Western Roman Emperor?
   a) Attila the Hun
   b) Odoacer
   c) Alaric I
   d) Theoderic the Great

4. What was the Byzantine Empire?
   a) The continuation of the Eastern Roman Empire
   b) A barbarian kingdom that replaced Rome
   c) A rival empire founded by Germanic tribes
   d) A medieval kingdom in Western Europe

5. Which Frankish ruler was crowned Emperor of the Romans in 800 AD?
   a) Clovis I
   b) Pepin the Short
   c) Charlemagne
   d) Louis the Pious

6. After the fall of the Western Roman Empire, which Germanic tribe created a kingdom in Italy and briefly maintained many Roman institutions?
   a) Vandals
   b) Ostrogoths
   c) Saxons
   d) Franks

7. Which former Roman province maintained many Roman laws and urban traditions well into the Middle Ages, thanks in part to the survival of the Byzantine Empire?
   a) Gaul
   b) Dacia
   c) Hispania
   d) Anatolia

8. What was the significance of the Battle of Tours in 732 AD?
   a) It marked the final fall of Rome
   b) It stopped the Viking invasion of England
   c) It halted the Muslim advance into Western Europe
   d) It led to the fall of Constantinople

9. Which scholar from Anglo-Saxon England helped preserve learning during the so-called Dark Ages?
   a) Thomas Aquinas
   b) Alcuin of York
   c) Geoffrey of Monmouth
   d) The Venerable Bede

10. What was the Holy Roman Empire?
    a) A direct continuation of the Roman Empire
    b) A medieval empire in Central Europe
    c) A Viking kingdom in Britain
    d) A Persian-led revival of Rome

11. What was the "Sub-Roman" period in Britain characterized by?
    a) Complete abandonment of Roman ways
    b) A sudden rise in Viking raids
    c) Survival of Roman customs mixed with local and Germanic influences
    d) An early conversion to Islam

12. What was the significance of the Corpus Juris Civilis, compiled under the Byzantine Emperor Justinian I?
    a) A history of Rome
    b) The first Christian Bible in Latin
    c) A codification of Roman law that influenced European legal systems
    d) A manual for medieval warfare

13. What significant cultural development took place in Ireland during the 6th–9th centuries, despite it never having been fully conquered by Rome?
    a) First feudal system
    b) Development of illuminated manuscripts like the Book of Kells
    c) Early gunpowder experiments
    d) First use of stirrups in battle

14. Who were the Moors?
    a) Scandinavian warriors who raided England
    b) Muslim rulers from North Africa who controlled Spain for centuries
    c) A Celtic tribe that resisted Roman conquest
    d) The ruling class of the Byzantine Empire

15. Which Celtic Christian monastery became a key intellectual hub in early medieval Europe, preserving Latin learning after Rome's fall?
    a) Cluny Abbey
    b) Lindisfarne
    c) Iona Abbey
    d) Monte Cassino

ANSWERS

1. **b) 476 AD** – Rome's fall is traditionally marked by the deposition of its last emperor, Romulus Augustulus, by Odoacer.

2. **b) Romulus Augustulus** – His name echoed both Rome's legendary founder (Romulus) and its first emperor (Augustus).

3. **b) Odoacer** – He ruled Italy but did not take the title of emperor.

4. **a) The continuation of the Eastern Roman Empire** – The Byzantine Empire lasted until 1453.

5. **c) Charlemagne** – Crowned by the Pope, he revived the idea of a Western Roman emperor.

6. **b) Ostrogoths** – The Ostrogoths, under Theodoric the Great, ruled Italy in the late 5th and early 6th centuries. They preserved many Roman institutions, allowed Roman senators to retain power, and patronized Roman culture—briefly blending Roman and Gothic rule.

7. **d) Anatolia** – Anatolia remained part of the Byzantine Empire, the eastern continuation of Rome. Cities like Constantinople thrived, preserving Roman law, urban life, and administration well into the Middle Ages.

8. **c) It halted the Muslim advance into Western Europe** – Charles Martel's victory preserved Christian rule in France.

9. **d) The Venerable Bede** – His historical writings helped preserve knowledge of early medieval Europe.

10. **b) A medieval empire in Central Europe** – The Holy Roman Empire was founded in 800 AD but was not a direct continuation of ancient Rome.

11. **c) Survival of Roman customs mixed with local and Germanic influences** – The Sub-Roman period in Britain (c. 410–600 CE) saw a fusion of Roman traditions, native Brittonic culture, and incoming Germanic (e.g., Anglo-Saxon) practices. Some towns remained inhabited, and Latin continued to be used in elite circles.

12. **c) A codification of Roman law that influenced European legal systems** – The Corpus Juris Civilis (Body of Civil Law) compiled under Justinian I in the 6th century was a monumental effort to preserve and systematize Roman legal knowledge. It later influenced medieval and modern European law.

13. **b) Development of illuminated manuscripts like the Book of Kells** – Irish monasteries created masterpieces like the Book of Kells (c. 800 CE), combining Christian themes with intricate Celtic design. Despite never being part of the Roman Empire, Ireland preserved and enhanced Latin literacy.

14. **b) Muslim rulers from North Africa who controlled Spain for centuries** – The Moors ruled much of Spain from 711 AD until 1492.

15. **c) Iona Abbey** – Founded by St. Columba in 563 CE, Iona became a center for religious scholarship and manuscript copying, playing a major role in preserving Latin learning and spreading Christianity in Scotland and northern England.

Conquest and Combat

Throughout the so-called Dark Ages, wars, invasions, and shifting empires defined history. From legendary knights to mysterious lost cities, the battlefields of medieval history hold countless secrets. Test your knowledge on the era's greatest conquests and warriors!

1. Which city was the largest in the world around the year 700 AD, with an estimated population of over one million?
   a) Rome
   b) London
   c) Constantinople
   d) Chang'an

2. The Moors ruled much of Spain for centuries. What was the name of their last stronghold before being defeated in 1492?
   a) Toledo
   b) Cordoba
   c) Granada
   d) Seville

3. The Knights Templar were originally founded for what purpose?
   a) Protecting Christian pilgrims traveling to the Holy Land
   b) Assassinating rival kings and rulers
   c) Overthrowing the Pope and taking control of the Church
   d) Defending the city of Constantinople

4. The Abbasid Caliphate moved the Islamic capital to which cosmopolitan city, which became a center for science, translation, and philosophy?
   a) Mecca
   b) Damascus
   c) Baghdad
   d) Cairo

5. What happened to the leader of the Knights Templar, Jacques de Molay, after the order was disbanded?
a) He escaped and lived in secrecy
b) He was burned at the stake
c) He was exiled to Jerusalem
d) He was assassinated by rival knights

6. Which Central Asian empire, flourishing in the 6th century, helped transmit Buddhism, silk, and diplomatic practices across the Silk Road?
a) Mongol Empire
b) Sassanid Empire
c) Sogdian Confederacy
d) Göktürk Khaganate

7. What was the elite Norse warrior unit that served as bodyguards to the Byzantine emperors?
a) The Janissaries
b) The Varangian Guard
c) The Templar Knights
d) The Black Army

8. Which medieval battle saw an outnumbered English army, using longbows, defeat a much larger French force in 1415?
a) The Battle of Tours
b) The Battle of Hastings
c) The Battle of Agincourt
d) The Battle of Poitiers

9. Which weapon, banned by the Church, was infamous for its brutal effectiveness in medieval combat?
a) The crossbow
b) The war hammer
c) The longsword
d) The flail

10. Which empire used elephants in battle, causing terror on medieval battlefields?
    a) The Byzantine Empire
    b) The Holy Roman Empire
    c) The Delhi Sultanate
    d) The Kingdom of Hungary

11. Which famous medieval weapon was designed to penetrate the heavy armor of knights by delivering a powerful, focused blow?
    a) The mace
    b) The crossbow
    c) The longbow
    d) The flail

12. Who was the feared Mongol general known for his ruthless campaigns across Persia and the Middle East?
    a) Hulagu Khan
    b) Kublai Khan
    c) Subutai
    d) Attila the Hun

13. Which Scottish rebel famously led a fight against English rule in the late 13th century?
    a) Robert the Bruce
    b) William Wallace
    c) Edward Balliol
    d) Owain Glyndŵr

14. Which legendary medieval knight supposedly survived over 50 battles, including fighting in both the Hundred Years' War and the Crusades?
    a) El Cid
    b) Bertrand du Guesclin
    c) Richard the Lionheart
    d) Jean de Dunois

15. Which deadly medieval fighting technique involved knights wrestling opponents to the ground and using daggers to pierce weak points in armor?
    a) Florentine fencing
    b) Half-swording
    c) The Schiavona method
    d) Mounted combat

ANSWER

1. **d) Chang'an** – Chang'an (modern Xi'an), capital of the Tang Dynasty, was the world's largest city around 700 AD, with over a million people. It was a multicultural hub, the eastern terminus of the Silk Road, and a model for later cities in East Asia.

2. **c) Granada** – The last stronghold of the Moors in Spain, Granada fell to Catholic monarchs Ferdinand and Isabella in 1492.

3. **a) Protecting Christian pilgrims traveling to the Holy Land** – The Templars originally served as bodyguards for travelers in the Crusader states.

4. **c) Baghdad** – Under the Abbasids, Baghdad (founded in 762 Ad) became a center of the Islamic Golden Age, with institutions like the House of Wisdom, where scholars translated texts from Greek, Sanskrit, and Persian into Arabic.

5. **b) He was burned at the stake** – Accused of heresy and burned at the stake, the Templars became the center of countless legends and conspiracy theories. Jacques de Molay, the last Grand Master of the Templars, was executed in 1314.

6. **d) Göktürk Khaganate** – The Göktürks, a Turkic nomadic empire, played a vital diplomatic and cultural role along the Silk Road, acting as intermediaries for Buddhism, Chinese goods, and even Byzantine envoys.

7. **b) The Varangian Guard** – These elite Norse warriors served as personal bodyguards to the Byzantine emperors.

8. **c) The Battle of Agincourt** – The English, led by Henry V, used longbows to defeat a much larger French army.

9. **a) The crossbow** – The Pope banned its use in Christian warfare in 1139 due to its deadly efficiency.

10. **c) The Delhi Sultanate** – Indian war elephants were a terrifying force on the battlefield.

11. **a) The mace** – A blunt weapon with a heavy head, it was effective at crushing plate armor and was widely used by knights and infantry during the Middle Ages.

12. **a) Hulagu Khan** – A grandson of Genghis Khan, he destroyed Baghdad in 1258 and wiped out the Abbasid Caliphate.

13. **b) William Wallace** – Immortalized in *Braveheart*, Wallace led Scotland's resistance against English rule.

14. **b) Bertrand du Guesclin** – A French knight, he fought in the Hundred Years' War and was one of the most skilled medieval warriors.

15. **b) Half-swording** – This technique allowed knights to grapple in close combat and use daggers or swords to exploit weaknesses in armor.

Plagues and Cures

Throughout history, plagues have shaped societies, collapsed empires, and fueled strange superstitions. From bizarre medieval remedies to quarantine measures that shaped the modern world, diseases have left an enduring mark on human civilization. How much do you know about the plagues of the past?

1. In 1521, the Diet of Worms was a pivotal moment in European history. What did it concern?
   a) The Black Death's legal ramifications
   b) The conquest of Mexico
   c) The condemnation of Martin Luther's writings
   d) The annexation of Bohemia by the Holy Roman Empire

2. Which bacterium is responsible for the Black Death?
   a) Yersinia pestis
   b) Bacillus anthracis
   c) Vibrio cholerae
   d) Clostridium botulinum

3. What was *not* a common (and completely ineffective) medieval treatment for the Black Death?
   a) Drinking gold-infused water
   b) Eating large amounts of garlic
   c) Sleeping on a bed of thorns
   d) Rubbing onions on infected sores

4. In what way did the Japanese city of Kyoto suffer in 1467 during the outbreak of the Ōnin War?
   a) It was swallowed by an earthquake
   b) It was sacked by Mongol raiders
   c) It burned for a decade, becoming a symbol of civil strife
   d) It was submerged in a massive tsunami

5. What iconic outfit did plague doctors wear in an attempt to protect themselves?
   a) A suit of armor
   b) A long cloak with a bird-like beak mask
   c) A white robe with a golden sun emblem
   d) An early haz-mat garment made of wicker

6. Which medieval city is credited with creating one of the first official quarantine systems?
   a) Paris
   b) Constantinople
   c) Venice
   d) Prague

7. How long was the original quarantine period for ships suspected of carrying the plague?
   a) 10 days
   b) 20 days
   c) 40 days
   d) 100 days

8. Which group was frequently scapegoated and accused of summoning the plague through dark magic?
   a) Witches
   b) Vampires
   c) Djinn
   d) Angels

9. What deadly disease devastated the Aztec Empire shortly before the Spanish conquest?
   a) Smallpox
   b) Bubonic plague
   c) Typhus
   d) Influenza

10. Which of these unusual "cures" was *not* believed to ward off the plague?
    a) Carrying a dead toad in your pocket
    b) Smelling flowers to purify the air
    c) Wearing shoes made of bread
    d) Drinking mercury as a tonic

11. Which pandemic helped bring an end to the Roman Empire by killing millions of people in the 6th century?
    a) The Black Death
    b) The Plague of Justinian
    c) The Spanish Flu
    d) The Antonine Plague

12. What was one of the biggest immediate social consequences of the Black Death in Europe?
    a) A sharp decline in religious faith
    b) A dramatic increase in wages for peasants
    c) The rise of witch hunts
    d) All of the above

13. Why did some people believe the plague was spread by Jewish communities, leading to violent massacres in the 14th century?
    a) Anti-Semitic rumors claimed they poisoned wells
    b) They had knowledge of medicine and suffered lower infection rates
    c) The Church accused them of summoning the disease
    d) All of the above

14. The Great Fire of 1567 destroyed two-thirds of which European city, sparking urban redevelopment and stricter building codes?
    a) Seville
    b) Edinburgh
    c) Lübeck
    d) London

15. Which bizarre medieval practice was meant to appease God and stop plagues?
    a) Self-flagellation (whipping oneself)
    b) Walking barefoot on hot coals
    c) Burning herbs in church altars
    d) Throwing coins into rivers for good luck

ANSWERS

1. **c) The condemnation of Martin Luther's writings** – At the Diet of Worms in 1521, Martin Luther was asked to recant his criticisms of the Catholic Church. He refused, famously saying, *"Here I stand."* It marked a decisive moment in the Protestant Reformation.

2. **a) Yersinia pestis** – This bacterium, carried by fleas on rats, was responsible for the pandemic.

3. **c) Sleeping on a bed of thorns** – While medieval people believed in suffering and penance as ways to appease divine wrath, this particular method was not a common plague remedy.

4. **c) It burned for a decade, becoming a symbol of civil strife** – The Ōnin War (1467–1477) devastated Kyoto, with constant factional fighting and fire. The city never fully recovered and it marked the beginning of the Sengoku period—a century of civil war in Japan.

5. **b) A long cloak with a bird-like beak mask** – The beak was filled with aromatic herbs, believed to filter out "bad air" (miasma).

6. **c) Venice** – In the 14th century, Venetian officials isolated ships for 40 days to prevent disease spread.

7. **c) 40 days** – The word "quarantine" comes from the Italian *quaranta giorni*, meaning "forty days."

8. **a) Witches** – Witchcraft accusations surged during outbreaks, with marginalized individuals (often women) blamed for "cursing" communities.

9. **a) Smallpox** – The Spanish brought smallpox to the Americas, devastating the Aztecs and other indigenous civilizations.

10. **c) Wearing shoes made of bread** – Unfortunately, drinking mercury was a real (though dangerous) historical remedy used for various diseases, including plague, syphilis, and more.

11. **b) The Plague of Justinian** – This early pandemic (541-542 AD) weakened the Byzantine Empire.

12. **b) A dramatic increase in wages for peasants** – The mass death toll from the Black Death led to severe labor shortages, which in turn forced landowners to offer higher wages to attract workers.

13. **d) All of the above** – Jews were falsely accused of poisoning wells and deliberately spreading disease, leading to massacres.

14. **b) Edinburgh** – In 1567, a massive fire in Edinburgh destroyed large portions of the city, leading to new building regulations and stone construction, a key phase in its urban development and part of broader Scottish urban reform.

15. **a) Self-flagellation (whipping oneself)** – Some groups believed beating themselves would atone for humanity's sins and stop the plague.

The Viking Discoveries

The Vikings were more than just fearsome raiders—they were also explorers, traders, and settlers who reached distant lands long before most of the world realized they existed. From North America to Russia, their voyages reshaped history, leaving behind myths, mysteries, and archaeological clues. How well do you know the real Viking explorers?

1. Which Viking explorer is credited with leading the first European voyage to North America?
   a) Erik the Red
   b) Leif Erikson
   c) Ragnar Lothbrok
   d) Harald Hardrada

2. What did the Vikings call the land they discovered in North America?
   a) Greenland
   b) Vinland
   c) Ultima Thule
   d) Svalbard

3. Where was the first confirmed Viking settlement in North America discovered?
   a) Newfoundland, Canada
   b) Maine, USA
   c) Iceland
   d) Nova Scotia, Canada

4. Which factor was *not* a primary reason Viking settlements in North America failed?
   a) Harsh winters
   b) Disease wiping out settlers
   c) Clashes with Indigenous peoples
   d) Isolation from Greenland

5. Which of the following did the Vikings *not* do?
   a) Raid European monasteries
   b) Establish settlements in North America
   c) Form the Holy Roman Empire
   d) Found the Duchy of Normandy

6. Which type of Norse poem preserved oral history and heroic deeds with complex metaphorical language known as kennings?
   a) Runes
   b) Skaldic poetry
   c) Saga prose
   d) Seiðr chants

7. What was the primary reason Vikings settled in Greenland?
   a) They were escaping a volcanic eruption in Iceland
   b) Greenland had rich farmlands and forests
   c) Erik the Red was exiled and needed a new home
   d) They discovered silver and gold there

8. The "Thing" in Viking society referred to what?
   a) A pagan fertility ritual
   b) A communal burial site
   c) An assembly for governance and law
   d) A long-distance raid

9. Why is the Vinland Map controversial?
   a) Some experts believe it is a modern forgery
   b) It contains names of places that shouldn't exist in the Viking era
   c) It was discovered in an unexpected location
   d) It uses ink that was unknown in medieval times

10. What Norse term was used to describe Indigenous peoples encountered in North America?
    a) Skraelings
    b) Thralls
    c) Jötnar
    d) Valkyries

11. Which of the following was a major Viking trading center, not primarily known as a raiding base?
    a) Birka
    b) Jorvik
    c) Dublin
    d) Reykjavik

12. Which precious material, highly valued by Vikings, was often collected from the shores of the North Atlantic?
    a) Amber
    b) Walrus ivory
    c) Obsidian
    d) Silk

13. Which modern country has the largest number of Viking ship burial sites?
    a) Denmark
    b) Iceland
    c) Norway
    d) Sweden

14. What was the "Danelaw"?
    a) A set of runic legal codes
    b) A Viking coinage system
    c) A territory in England governed under Norse law
    d) A Norse oath of loyalty to Danish kings

15. What happened to the Viking settlements in Greenland?
    a) They were destroyed by Indigenous attacks
    b) Climate change made survival difficult
    c) They were conquered by the English
    d) A volcanic eruption forced them to flee

ANSWERS

1. **b) Leif Erikson** – Around the year 1000 AD, Leif Erikson sailed to what he called Vinland, likely part of modern-day Canada.

2. **b) Vinland** – The name suggests a land of vines or fertile pastures, although its exact meaning is debated.

3. **a) Newfoundland, Canada** – The Viking site at L'Anse aux Meadows provides archaeological proof of Norse presence.

4. **b) Disease wiping out settlers** – Unlike later European colonizers, the Norse did not suffer mass plague deaths. Conflicts, climate, and logistics were the key factors.

5. **c) Form the Holy Roman Empire** – Vikings raided and settled widely but were not involved in founding the Holy Roman Empire.

6. **b) Skaldic poetry** – Skaldic poetry was composed by skalds, court poets who used elaborate language and kennings (e.g., "whale-road" for sea) to immortalize kings, battles, and myths in Norse society.

7. **c) Erik the Red was exiled and needed a new home** – He convinced other Norse settlers to follow him there.

8. **c) An assembly for governance and law** – The Thing was a democratic assembly where Vikings settled disputes, created laws, and made decisions—an early form of participatory governance.

9. **a) Some experts believe it is a modern forgery** – The ink used in the Vinland Map, A controversial map that supposedly shows Viking knowledge of North America before Columbus, has been questioned by scientists.

10. **a) Skraelings** – This was the Viking term for the Indigenous peoples they encountered.

11. **a) Birka** – Located in Sweden, Birka was a cosmopolitan trade center that connected Scandinavia to the wider world, including the Byzantine Empire and Islamic Caliphates, through goods like furs, silver, and amber.

12. **b) Walrus ivory** – It was a luxury material used for art, game pieces, and trade.

13. **c) Norway** – Many iconic Viking ship burial sites (as well as ruins and artifacts) have been found in Norway.

14. **c) A territory in England governed under Norse law** – The Danelaw was a part of Anglo-Saxon England where Danish and Norse laws and customs prevailed—roughly covering the north and east, including cities like York (Jorvik) and Lincoln.

15. **b) Climate change made survival difficult** – A cooling period, combined with isolation, led to their disappearance.

Religious Upheavals

The medieval world was shaped by faith, but religious beliefs were also a source of conflict, rebellion, and persecution. From heretical movements and brutal inquisitions to mysterious crusades, the era was marked by upheaval and change. How well do you know the strange and shocking religious events of the past?

1. Who were the Cathars, and why were they persecuted?
   a) A sect of warrior monks who opposed the Pope
   b) A Christian movement in France deemed heretical
   c) A secretive Jewish-Christian brotherhood
   d) A pagan group resisting conversion

2. Which European country is believed to have executed the highest number of accused witches in the early modern period?
   a) England
   b) Italy
   c) Germany
   d) France

3. Which medieval Islamic philosopher's commentaries on Aristotle had a major impact on Christian scholastic thinkers like Thomas Aquinas?
   a) Al-Ghazali
   b) Ibn Sina (Avicenna)
   c) Ibn Rushd (Averroes)
   d) Al-Farabi

4. The Synod of Whitby (664 AD) was convened in Anglo-Saxon England to resolve what issue?
   a) Use of Latin vs. vernacular in church services
   b) The correct date of Easter
   c) Female ordination
   d) Whether icons were allowed in churches

5. Which famous religious schism in 1054 split Christianity into Eastern Orthodox and Roman Catholic branches?
   a) The Investiture Controversy
   b) The Great Schism
   c) The Avignon Crisis
   d) The Reformation

6. What controversial practice did the medieval Waldensians promote, leading to their persecution as heretics?
   a) Advocating for the abolition of the priesthood
   b) Publicly burning Bibles to protest Church corruption
   c) Performing secret pagan rituals in churches
   d) Claiming the Pope was the Antichrist

7. In medieval Japan, the Buddhist concept of mappō became widespread. What did it mean?
   a) A rejection of all Buddhist doctrine
   b) They felt it was a golden age of spiritual enlightenment
   c) They felt it was time of moral and spiritual decline
   d) Reincarnation into the animal realm

8. What was the primary reason the Knights Templar were persecuted and disbanded?
   a) Accusations of blasphemy and secret rituals
   b) A failed attempt to conquer Jerusalem
   c) Their opposition to the Pope
   d) The rise of a rival order, the Hospitallers

9. What was the *Pardoner's* role in the medieval Church, as criticized by Chaucer in *The Canterbury Tales*?
   a) A priest who heard confessions
   b) A monk who copied texts
   c) A seller of indulgences
   d) A missionary to non-Christian lands

10. What unusual practice did flagellants perform during the 14th century, especially during the time of the Black Death?
    a) Public fasting for 40 days
    b) Marching barefoot across Europe
    c) Self-whipping in public processions
    d) Silent vigils on mountaintops

11. Who was burned at the stake in 1431 for heresy, later becoming a saint?
    a) Joan of Arc
    b) Catherine of Siena
    c) Margery Kempe
    d) Hildegard of Bingen

12. Which group of people were also frequently accused of witchcraft, especially in continental Europe, contrary to the stereotypes?
    a) Clergy
    b) Midwives
    c) Children
    d) Men

13. What role did the Spanish Inquisition play in religious upheaval?
    a) It sought to enforce Catholic orthodoxy and suppress heresy
    b) It defended religious freedom across Europe
    c) It worked to unite Catholic and Orthodox Christians
    d) It primarily focused on stopping the Protestant Reformation

14. What was the "Dance of Death," often depicted in medieval religious art?
    a) A secret ritual of the Cathars
    b) A warning about the universality of death
    c) A pagan festival adapted by Christians
    d) A practice performed by plague doctors

15. What happened to Martin Luther after he challenged the Catholic Church with his 95 Theses?
    a) He was executed as a heretic
    b) He was excommunicated but survived under noble protection
    c) He became Pope in a later reform movement
    d) He renounced his beliefs and returned to the Church

ANSWERS

1. **b) A Christian movement in France deemed heretical** – The Cathars believed in a dualistic world of good and evil, which clashed with Catholic doctrine.

2. **c) Germany** – What is now Germany saw more witch trials and executions than any other region—estimates suggest up to 25,000 people were killed, especially in the fragmented Holy Roman Empire, where local lords had legal control.

3. **c) Ibn Rushd (Averroes)** – His works were translated into Latin and became central to medieval European debates about faith and reason, earning him the epithet "The Commentator" in scholastic circles.

4. **b) The correct date of Easter** – The Synod of Whitby was called to decide whether to follow the Celtic or Roman method of calculating Easter. King Oswiu of Northumbria chose the Roman practice, aligning English Christianity more closely with continental Europe.

5. **b) The Great Schism** – In 1054, the Christian Church formally split into the Roman Catholic and Eastern Orthodox Churches.

6. **a) Advocating for the abolition of the priesthood** – The Waldensians (12th century) emphasized lay preaching, vernacular Bible translations, and rejection of clerical authority. Their defiance of the Church's hierarchy led to their condemnation as heretics.

7. **c) A time of moral and spiritual decline** – In Japanese Pure Land Buddhism, mappō refers to the degenerate age of the Dharma, when people could no longer achieve enlightenment through traditional practices. It led to an emphasis on faith in Amida Buddha and salvation through chanting his name.

8. **a) Accusations of blasphemy and secret rituals** – Though likely false, these charges justified dissolving the wealthy order.

9. **c) A seller of indulgences** – In *The Canterbury Tales*, Chaucer's Pardoner is a hypocritical character who sells indulgences—pardons from punishment for sins. The corruption of such practices later fueled Martin Luther's Reformation.

10. **c) Self-whipping in public processions** – Flagellants believed that public self-punishment would earn God's mercy during times of plague and crisis. They marched through towns whipping themselves, often chanting prayers. The Church condemned them for promoting unregulated religious fervor.

11. **a) Joan of Arc** – The French heroine was accused of heresy and burned at the stake before being canonized centuries later.

12. **d) Men** – While about 75–80% of the accused were women, thousands of men—especially hermits, healers, and foreigners—were also accused. In some regions (e.g. Iceland), men were the majority of the accused.

13. **a) It sought to enforce Catholic orthodoxy and suppress heresy** – The Spanish Inquisition targeted Jews, Muslims, and suspected heretics.

14. **b) A warning about the universality of death** – The "Danse Macabre" reminded people that death spared no one, rich or poor.

15. **b) He was excommunicated but survived under noble protection** – Luther's ideas sparked the Protestant Reformation, forever changing Christianity.

Final Score: How Did You Do?

- 60–75 correct: Historical Hero
- 45–59 correct: Seasoned Scholar
- 30–44 correct: Time-Travel Trainee
- 15–29 correct: Trivia Tourist
- 0–14 correct: Chronologically Confused

THE RENAISSANCE AND BEYOND – THE RISE OF THE CURIOUS

The world was stirring. Across sunlit workshops, bustling ports, and dusty libraries, a new hunger for knowledge began to spread—a bold curiosity that defied old boundaries and dared to imagine a world beyond the horizon. This was a time of thinkers and dreamers, explorers and questioners, all restless to uncover hidden truths and push beyond the familiar. Whether on land or sea, in great cities or quiet villages, people of every walk of life found themselves swept up in a tide of discovery that promised to reshape the world forever.

But not all revolutions are written in grand books or painted on vaulted ceilings. Beneath the glow of celebrated genius, countless untold stories unfolded—stories of everyday lives, secret societies, forgotten maps, and ideas whispered in the corners of history. In this chapter, you'll step into that rich, complex world, where curiosity was both a compass and a torch.

Did you know...?

In 1518, a mysterious "dancing plague" broke out in Strasbourg, where dozens of people began dancing uncontrollably in the streets. Some reportedly danced for days without rest, and a few even died from exhaustion or stroke. Historians still debate the cause—was it mass hysteria, ergot poisoning from moldy grain, or a stress-induced psychosis? Whatever the reason, it remains one of the strangest public health events of the Renaissance.

The Hidden Lives of Peasants

When we think of the Renaissance, we often picture grand cathedrals, famous artists, and powerful rulers. But what about the ordinary people who lived in villages and towns, working the land, raising families, and celebrating life in their own way? Let's uncover the lesser-known stories of peasants and everyday folk during this fascinating era.

1. What percentage of the population were peasants during the Renaissance?
   a) 10-20%
   b) 30-40%
   c) 70-90%
   d) Less than 5%

2. What every day object became a major symbol of status and fashion among Renaissance urban dwellers?
   a) Fork
   b) Handkerchief
   c) Hat
   d) Mirror

3. What was the purpose of sumptuary laws in Renaissance Europe?
   a) To prevent peasants from learning to read
   b) To regulate what people could wear based on their social class
   c) To limit the number of farm animals a family could own
   d) To enforce mandatory religious attendance

4. What unusual job involved collecting a specific creature for medical treatments?
   a) Rat herder
   b) Leech collector
   c) Crow whisperer
   d) Flea tamer

5. What was one of the most common forms of peasant entertainment?
   a) Watching plays in grand theaters
   b) Attending public executions
   c) Playing chess and reading novels
   d) Watching jousting tournaments

6. Which drink was often safer to consume than water for peasants?
   a) Coffee
   b) Beer
   c) Wine
   d) Goat's milk

7. Which non-European empire experienced a significant cultural and scientific renaissance at the same time as Europe's?
   a) Mughal Empire
   b) Aztec Empire
   c) Songhai Empire
   d) Inca Empire

8. Which of the following was a real festival celebrated by peasants?
   a) The Feast of Fools
   b) The Festival of Moonlight
   c) The Night of the Witches
   d) The Harvest Jamboree

9. What type of "Renaissance man" was Paracelsus, the controversial Swiss figure of the 16th century?
   a) A comedian and politician
   b) A poet-king
   c) A scientist-alchemist-healer
   d) A spy and playwright

10. What was a "fart catcher" in medieval and Renaissance times?
    a) A nobleman's servant who aired out rooms
    b) A court jester specializing in rude humor
    c) A padded cushion used in place of chairs
    d) A nickname for chimney sweeps

11. Which of the following was *not* a common form of punishment for minor crimes in villages?
    a) Being put in the stocks
    b) A public whipping
    c) Wearing a crown of thorns
    d) Having to wear a shame mask

12. Why did many peasants only bathe a few times a year?
    a) They believed it would make them sick
    b) Soap was too expensive
    c) They didn't have time due to farming duties
    d) They only bathed on holy days

13. What was a "sin-eater" in Renaissance folklore?
    a) A person who claimed to absorb the sins of the dead
    b) A priest who performed last rites
    c) A doctor who treated diseases with prayers
    d) A term for people who fasted for religious reasons

14. Which 15th-century invention had the most profound effect on the daily lives and education of ordinary Europeans?
    a) Mechanical clock
    b) Printing press
    c) Paper money
    d) Compass

15. What was the main reason Renaissance peasants participated in revolts?
    a) Heavy taxation and unfair treatment
    b) To gain voting rights
    c) Religious disagreements with the Church
    d) To protest against foreign settlers arriving in their cities

---

ANSWERS

1. **c) 70-90%** – Most of the population were peasants, working on farms and in villages under the rule of lords and monarchs.

2. **a) Fork** – The fork, once viewed as decadent and foreign, became a symbol of sophistication during the Renaissance. It was especially favored in Italy and among the upper classes by the late 16th century.

3. **b) To regulate what people could wear based on their social class** – Sumptuary laws dictated that only nobles could wear certain colors and fabrics like silk or purple dye.

4. **b) Leech collector** – Leeches were used in medical bloodletting practices, and some people made a living gathering them.

5. **b) Attending public executions** – These grim events were major social gatherings, often treated as entertainment.

6. **b) Beer** – Low-alcohol beer and ale was safer to drink than untreated water, which was often contaminated, but the idea that peasants drank beer exclusively is a myth. Water was also consumed, and beer was not always safer or more available

7. **c) Songhai Empire** – The Songhai Empire in West Africa (particularly under Askia the Great) experienced a golden

age of learning, especially in Timbuktu, where Islamic scholarship and science flourished alongside trade.

8. **a) The Feast of Fools** – A festival where social order was humorously reversed, and peasants could mock authorities.

9. **c) A scientist-alchemist-healer** – Paracelsus rejected the ancient medical teachings of Galen and promoted new ideas based on chemical remedies and observation, blending alchemy, medicine, and mysticism. He laid the groundwork for toxicology.

10. **a) A nobleman's servant who aired out rooms** – Some households employed servants to ensure rooms smelled fresh.

11. **c) Wearing a crown of thorns** – Although a symbol from religious tradition, wearing a crown of thorns was not part of village punishments for petty crimes.

12. **a) They believed it would make them sick** – Many thought bathing too often could open the body to disease.

13. **a) A person who claimed to absorb the sins of the dead** – Sin-eaters were paid to ritually "consume" the sins of deceased people.

14. **b) Printing press** – Invented by Johannes Gutenberg around 1440, the printing press revolutionized access to books, literacy, and the spread of ideas—making knowledge available beyond the elite for the first time in history.

15. **a) Heavy taxation and unfair treatment** – Many peasant revolts, like the English Peasants' Revolt of 1381, were driven by economic hardship.

The Seven Seas

For centuries, humanity has ventured across the vast oceans, discovering new lands, waging wars, and pushing the boundaries of maritime technology. From legendary explorers to infamous pirates, the history of the sea is filled with adventure, mystery, and groundbreaking innovation.

1. Which ancient civilization is credited with inventing the first true ocean-going ships?
   a) The Egyptians
   b) The Phoenicians
   c) The Greeks
   d) The Romans

2. What was unique about the Chinese explorer Zheng He's fleet in the 15th century?
   a) His ships were among the largest wooden ships ever built
   b) He discovered North America before Columbus
   c) He was the first to circumnavigate the globe
   d) His fleet was made entirely of iron

3. Which famous lost naval fleet disappeared in a storm while attempting to invade Japan?
   a) The Spanish Armada
   b) The Byzantine Ghost Fleet
   c) The Mongol Invasion Fleet
   d) The Persian Royal Navy

4. What was the main reason the Spanish Armada failed in its invasion of England in 1588?
   a) A surprise counterattack by the Vikings
   b) A devastating storm and English naval tactics
   c) Sabotage from within the Spanish fleet
   d) A rebellion in Spain that caused the fleet to turn back

5. Who was known as the most successful pirate in history, commanding hundreds of ships?
   a) Blackbeard
   b) Henry Morgan
   c) Ching Shih
   d) Sir Francis Drake

6. What deadly disease was the biggest killer of sailors during the Age of Exploration?
   a) Cholera
   b) Scurvy
   c) Smallpox
   d) Malaria

7. What was a major technological advantage of Renaissance-era naval warfare?
   a) The use of metal-clad ships
   b) The development of the cannon-armed galleon
   c) Steam-powered warships
   d) Submarines equipped with torpedoes

8. Which ancient culture is believed to have crossed the Pacific Ocean long before European explorers?
   a) The Aztecs
   b) The Polynesians
   c) The Vikings
   d) The Mayans

9. What unusual method did some pirates use to intimidate their enemies?
   a) Carrying a live shark on deck
   b) Setting their own ships on fire
   c) Wearing elaborate red silk coats
   d) Flying deceptive or false flags

10. Which famous naval battle saw the destruction of an entire fleet in a single day?
    a) The Battle of Salamis (480 BCE)
    b) The Battle of Trafalgar (1805)
    c) The Battle of Lepanto (1571)
    d) The Battle of Tsushima (1905)

11. What was a common superstition among sailors in the past?
    a) Whistling on board would summon storms
    b) Eating fish would bring bad luck
    c) Seeing dolphins meant disaster was near
    d) Painting the ship red would keep away spirits

12. What group of sailors terrorized the North African coast and enslaved thousands of Europeans during the 16th and 17th centuries?
    a) Ottoman Janissaries
    b) Moorish pirates
    c) Barbary corsairs
    d) Mamluks

13. Which European power dominated global sea trade during the 17th century?
    a) Spain
    b) Portugal
    c) The Netherlands
    d) England

14. What innovative ship design, developed by the Portuguese in the 15th century, enabled longer sea voyages and helped kick off the Age of Exploration?
    a) Galley
    b) Cog
    c) Junk
    d) Caravel

15. What mysterious lost fleet vanished in the Bermuda Triangle in 1918?
    a) The USS Cyclops
    b) The Franklin Expedition
    c) The Flying Dutchman Fleet
    d) The Spanish Silver Convoy

ANSWERS

1. **b) The Phoenicians** – These master sailors built sturdy ships and dominated Mediterranean trade for centuries.

2. **a) His ships were among the largest wooden ships ever built** – Zheng He's treasure ships were enormous. Size estimates of these ships vary from 200 feet to a whopping 400 feet in length.

3. **c) The Mongol Invasion Fleet** – Kublai Khan sent two major fleets to invade Japan, both of which were destroyed by typhoons, known as the "kamikaze" or "divine wind."

4. **b) A devastating storm and English naval tactics** – The Spanish Armada was hit by a storm and harassed by smaller, more maneuverable English ships.

5. **c) Ching Shih** – A powerful pirate queen of China who led thousands of sailors and controlled a vast fleet.

6. **b) Scurvy** – A lack of vitamin C led to this deadly disease, causing weakness, bleeding gums, and death.

7. **b) The development of the cannon-armed galleon** – These heavily armed ships changed naval warfare by allowing long-range bombardments.

8. **b) The Polynesians** – These skilled navigators traveled vast distances across the Pacific using stars and ocean currents.

9. **d) Flying deceptive or false flags** – Pirates often raised friendly flags to trick merchant ships before attacking.

10. **a) The Battle of Salamis** – In 480 BCE, the Greek navy defeated the much larger Persian fleet in a single day.

11. **a) Whistling on board would summon storms** – Many sailors believed whistling could anger the wind gods.

12. **c) Barbary corsairs** – Operating from North African ports like Algiers and Tunis, these pirates captured European ships and coastal villages, selling captives into slavery. European powers often paid ransoms or launched retaliatory attacks.

13. **c) The Netherlands** – The Dutch East India Company controlled trade routes and was one of the most powerful maritime empires.

14. **d) Caravel** – The caravel was a nimble ship with lateen sails, allowing it to sail against the wind. It was instrumental for Portuguese exploration down the African coast and eventually across the Atlantic.

15. **a) The USS Cyclops** – This massive U.S. Navy ship disappeared in the Bermuda Triangle in 1918 with over 300 men aboard.

Patronage and the Power of Art

Step into the dazzling world of the Renaissance — a time of artistic genius, daring ideas, and cultural rebirth. From the powerful patrons of Florence to the trailblazing women who defied societal norms, this era reshaped how humans understood art, knowledge, and themselves. Test your knowledge of the people, cities, and creative sparks that lit up this extraordinary period.

1. What economic innovation began to reappear in former Roman areas during the Carolingian Renaissance under Charlemagne?
    a) Use of coinage and standardized weights
    b) Bartering with shells
    c) Silk trade with China
    d) Slave markets in Italy

2. Which female Renaissance writer's proto-feminist work *The Book of the City of Ladies* challenged misogynistic narratives of the time?
    a) Sofonisba Anguissola
    b) Isotta Nogarola
    c) Christine de Pizan
    d) Laura Cereta

3. What Renaissance city became renowned for its printing industry and housed one of the largest publishing houses in Europe, run by Aldus Manutius?
    a) Florence
    b) Venice
    c) Paris
    d) Antwerp

4. Who was the Renaissance playwright whose plays predated Shakespeare and introduced blank verse to English drama?
   a) Thomas Kyd
   b) Ben Jonson
   c) Christopher Marlowe
   d) John Lyly

5. The Ottonian Renaissance took place primarily in which modern country?
   a) France
   b) Italy
   c) Germany
   d) Spain

6. What was one major artistic contribution of the Ottonian Renaissance?
   a) The revival of monumental buildings
   b) The development of perspective painting
   c) The return of classical Greek sculpture
   d) The first Gothic cathedrals

7. Which Renaissance city was known for its republican politics, textile wealth, and for being the cradle of early Renaissance art and architecture?
   a) Naples
   b) Bruges
   c) Florence
   d) Rome

8. What was the *commedia dell'arte*, a popular form of Renaissance theatre in Italy?
   a) A tragic monologue form
   b) A religious mystery play
   c) An improvised comedy with stock characters
   d) A poetic epic performed by nobles

9. What major event helped trigger the Renaissance of the 12th century?
   a) The discovery of America
   b) The Crusades and rediscovery of Greek and Arabic knowledge
   c) The fall of the Byzantine Empire
   d) The Black Death

10. Which language became the dominant scholarly language during these earlier renaissances?
    a) Greek
    b) Latin
    c) Arabic
    d) French

11. What was the role of Muslim scholars in preserving ancient knowledge?
    a) They hid the most ancient manuscripts
    b) They translated and preserved Greek and Roman texts
    c) They banned the study of modern knowledge
    d) They rewrote classical texts to reflect Islamic teachings

12. Which Renaissance artist and engineer designed stage sets and theatrical effects for court productions, combining art and mechanical design?
    a) Raphael
    b) Leonardo da Vinci
    c) Bramante
    d) Titian

13. Which Renaissance painting includes a rare depiction of a woman (hypothetically Hypatia or another ancient philosopher) among male philosophers in a classical setting?
    a) Primavera – Botticelli
    b) The Ambassadors – Holbein
    c) The School of Athens – Raphael
    d) The Last Supper – Leonardo da Vinci

14. Who was the female Renaissance artist praised by Michelangelo, and whose self-portraits subtly challenged gender norms of the time?
    a) Lavinia Fontana
    b) Plautilla Nelli
    c) Artemisia Gentileschi
    d) Sofonisba Anguissola

15. Who was the female scholar from Verona known for her theological debates and Latin writings in the 15th century?
    a) Isotta Nogarola
    b) Hildegard of Bingen
    c) Vittoria Colonna
    d) Anne Askew

ANSWERS

1. **a) Use of coinage and standardized weights** – During the Carolingian Renaissance, there was a revival of literacy, legal reform, and economic standardization, including the reintroduction of coinage, which helped stabilize trade in former Roman territories.

2. **c) Christine de Pizan** – Christine de Pizan, writing in the early 15th century, authored *The Book of the City of Ladies*, defending women's intellectual and moral capacities. She is considered one of the first feminist writers in Europe.

3. **b) Venice** – Venice became a printing hub in the Renaissance. Aldus Manutius revolutionized the book industry with italic type and portable editions, turning Venice into a center for intellectual exchange and humanist scholarship.

4. **c) Christopher Marlowe** – Marlowe was a pioneer of blank verse and his plays, like *Doctor Faustus* and *Tamburlaine*, helped shape English Renaissance drama before Shakespeare rose to prominence.

5. **c) Germany** – The Ottonian Renaissance occurred under the rule of the Ottonian Dynasty in the Holy Roman Empire.

6. **a) The revival of monumental buildings** – Ottonian architects revived large stone buildings with intricate decorations. This laid the groundwork for Romanesque architecture, which flourished after the Ottonian period.

7. **c) Florence** – Florence was a beacon of Renaissance culture, due to its wealthy merchant class (especially the Medici), its semi-republican governance, and its investments in art and architecture.

8. **c) An improvised comedy with stock characters** – *Commedia dell'arte* was an unscripted, mask-based performance style featuring recurring characters like Arlecchino (Harlequin) and Pantalone, laying the groundwork for modern slapstick and sitcom archetypes.

9. **b) The Crusades and rediscovery of Greek and Arabic knowledge** – Contact with the Islamic world reintroduced lost classical works.

10. **b) Latin** – It remained the language of scholarship and learning for centuries.

11. **b) They translated and preserved Greek and Roman texts** – Scholars like Avicenna and Averroes kept classical knowledge alive.

12. **b) Leonardo da Vinci** – Leonardo designed elaborate mechanical devices for plays and court festivals, including movable scenery and flying machines, blending his artistic vision with scientific invention.

13. **c) The School of Athens – Raphael** – This fresco, painted in the Vatican, includes one female figure — possibly Hypatia or a symbolic muse — subtly inserted into a sea of male philosophers. Raphael may have done this at the urging of his patron or in homage to female intellect.

14. **d) Sofonisba Anguissola** – A court painter for the Spanish crown, Sofonisba created nuanced self-portraits that played with societal expectations and impressed even Michelangelo, who mentored her briefly.

15. **a) Isotta Nogarola** – Isotta was a renowned female humanist scholar who corresponded with major intellectuals of her day and debated issues like original sin and gender. She was a rare example of a woman in the male-dominated world of Renaissance scholarship.

Intellectual Movements and Secret Societies

The Renaissance was not only a time of artistic and scientific flourishing but also an era of hidden knowledge, secretive organizations, and lost wisdom. From the destruction of ancient libraries to the influence of secret societies, history is filled with mysteries that continue to spark curiosity today.

1. Which Renaissance figure's anatomical drawings, based on human dissection, were not published until centuries after his death, despite their extraordinary accuracy?
   a) Andreas Vesalius
   b) Leonardo da Vinci
   c) Ambroise Paré
   d) Paracelsus

2. What was supposedly lost in the destruction of the Library of Alexandria?
   a) The original texts of Plato and Aristotle
   b) A complete map of the world
   c) Evidence of alien contact
   d) The formula for the Philosopher's Stone

3. Which Renaissance-era manuscript remains one of history's most mysterious undeciphered texts?
   a) The Voynich Manuscript
   b) The Gutenberg Bible
   c) The Codex Gigas
   d) The Emerald Tablet

4. What is the Freemasons' connection to the Renaissance?
   a) The order was founded in the 1500s by Leonardo da Vinci
   b) They preserved secret mathematical and architectural knowledge
   c) They built the Vatican's Sistine Chapel
   d) Originally an underground military organization

5. Which famous scientist was suspected of being an alchemist?
   a) Galileo Galilei
   b) Isaac Newton
   c) Nicolaus Copernicus
   d) Johannes Kepler

6. The Rosicrucians first appeared in the early 17th century, but what did they claim?
   a) They had existed for centuries in secret
   b) They discovered a lost civilization
   c) They were in contact with extraterrestrial beings
   d) They could turn lead into gold

7. What was the primary goal of alchemists during the Renaissance?
   a) Creating life from inanimate objects
   b) Achieving immortality and discovering the Philosopher's Stone
   c) Building cathedrals with divine proportions
   d) Communicating with spirits

8. Who coined the phrase "the father of modern science" for his work in physics, astronomy, and the scientific method?
   a) Francis Bacon
   b) Tycho Brahe
   c) Galileo Galilei
   d) Johannes Kepler

9. Which Renaissance thinker challenged the four-element theory of matter and proposed that matter was made of chemical substances governed by reactions?
   a) Robert Boyle
   b) Paracelsus
   c) Avicenna
   d) Roger Bacon

10. Who were the Cathars, and why were they considered dangerous?
    a) A sect accused of witchcraft and alchemy
    b) A religious group that rejected Catholic Church authority
    c) A secret group of Renaissance architects
    d) A society of hidden mathematicians

11. Which secretive organization was disbanded by Pope Clement V in 1312 but rumored to have survived?
    a) The Jesuits
    b) The Knights Templar
    c) The Illuminati
    d) The Rosicrucians

12. What was the Emerald Tablet, according to legend?
    a) A text containing the secrets of alchemy
    b) A map to the lost city of Atlantis
    c) A book of prophecies about the end of the world
    d) A medieval recipe for immortality

13. What Renaissance codebreaker and occultist wrote about "angelic language" and mystical communication?
    a) John Dee
    b) Niccolò Machiavelli
    c) Francis Bacon
    d) Paracelsus

14. What rare astronomical event in 1524 caused widespread panic across Europe due to astrological predictions of floods and doom?
    a) Solar eclipse during Easter
    b) Jupiter-Saturn conjunction
    c) A great planetary conjunction in Pisces
    d) Meteor shower over Florence

15. What is the most famous hidden message supposedly encoded in a Renaissance painting?
    a) A musical score hidden in The Last Supper
    b) A secret map to a lost treasure in the Mona Lisa
    c) A prophecy of the Black Death in Botticelli's works
    d) A hidden star chart in Michelangelo's frescoes

ANSWERS

1. **b) Leonardo da Vinci** – Da Vinci's anatomical drawings, based on meticulous dissections, remained unpublished during his lifetime. They were more accurate than many medical texts of the time and prefigured later advances in understanding human anatomy.

2. **a) The original texts of Plato and Aristotle** – Many works from ancient Greek and Egyptian scholars were lost. However, it is not possible to say with certainty which specific texts vanished. Bizarrely, some believe they were secretly preserved in the Vatican Archives and secret collections.

3. **a) The Voynich Manuscript** – A mysterious book filled with unknown symbols and bizarre illustrations which has not yet been deciphered.

4. **b) They preserved secret mathematical and architectural knowledge** – The Freemasons evolved from medieval stonemason guilds.

5. **b) Isaac Newton** – Newton spent years studying alchemy alongside his scientific discoveries.

6. **a) They had existed for centuries in secret** – Rosicrucians claimed ancient origins, though their first texts appeared in the 1600s.

7. **b) Achieving immortality and discovering the Philosopher's Stone** – Alchemists sought both eternal life and the transmutation of metals.

8. **c) Galileo Galilei** – Galileo is often dubbed "the father of modern science" for his empirical approach, development of the scientific method, and use of the telescope to support heliocentrism (the movement of Earth around the sun).

9. **b) Paracelsus** – Paracelsus rejected the classical four-element theory (earth, water, air, fire) and introduced the concept of chemical medicine, emphasizing substances like sulfur, mercury, and salt as foundational to matter and disease.

10. **b) A religious group that rejected Catholic Church authority** – The Cathars were seen as heretics and were wiped out in the 13th century.

11. **b) The Knights Templar** – Officially disbanded, they became the center of conspiracy theories.

12. **a) A text containing the secrets of alchemy** – The Emerald Tablet was a legendary work said to contain the key to transmutation.

13. **a) John Dee** – A mathematician, astrologer, and adviser to Queen Elizabeth I, he developed a mystical system called Enochian magic.

14. **c) A great planetary conjunction in Pisces** – The 1524 conjunction of most major planets in Pisces, a water sign, was interpreted by astrologers as a sign of a cataclysmic flood. It led to mass panic, especially in German-speaking regions.

15. **a) A musical score hidden in The Last Supper** – Some researchers believe Da Vinci encoded musical notes into his famous painting.

The Age of Exploration

The Age of Exploration was a time of daring voyages, mysterious maps, and forgotten discoveries that shaped the world as we know it today. However, many stories remain untold—lost cities, overlooked explorers, and ancient knowledge that challenges conventional narratives. How much do you know about this thrilling era?

1. Which ancient map suggests that early civilizations may have had knowledge of Antarctica long before its "official" discovery?
   a) The Piri Reis Map
   b) The Vinland Map
   c) The Tabula Rogeriana
   d) The Fra Mauro Map

2. What deadly and unanticipated consequence followed Vasco da Gama's arrival in India in 1498?
   a) Introduction of syphilis
   b) Collapse of the spice trade
   c) Naval warfare with Arab merchants
   d) Spread of European influenza

3. What is one reason why the "discovery" of America by Columbus is misleading?
   a) The Vikings had already settled parts of North America centuries earlier
   b) Columbus landed in India, not America
   c) He was actually searching for Africa, not the New World
   d) His ships were blown off course, and he never meant to explore

4. Which lost city of gold was sought after by explorers but never found?
   a) El Dorado
   b) Shangri-La
   c) Atlantis
   d) Timbuktu

5. Which Muslim explorer traveled over 75,000 miles and documented his journeys across Africa, the Middle East, and Asia?
   a) Ibn Battuta
   b) Al-Idrisi
   c) Zheng He
   d) Vasco da Gama

6. Which European power established the first global maritime trading empire, spanning from Brazil to Japan by the mid-16th century?
   a) Spain
   b) Portugal
   c) England
   d) The Netherlands

7. What was the original goal of Magellan's expedition before he was killed?
   a) To prove the Earth was round
   b) To find a westward route to the Spice Islands
   c) To claim new lands for Portugal
   d) To convert indigenous peoples to Christianity

8. What major problem did early European explorers face when sailing into unknown waters?
   a) Lack of knowledge about ocean currents
   b) Compasses didn't work near the equator
   c) They feared sea monsters would attack their ships
   d) The maps they had were too detailed and confusing

9. What was one reason why Timbuktu became legendary in the Age of Exploration?
   a) It was said to have streets paved with gold
   b) It was a great center of trade and scholarship in Africa
   c) It was home to the largest standing army in the world
   d) It was the last remaining city of the Roman Empire

10. Which European explorer mysteriously vanished while searching for the fabled Northwest Passage?
    a) Henry Hudson
    b) John Cabot
    c) Ferdinand Magellan
    d) Francisco Pizarro

11. What was unique about the Fra Mauro Map created in the 15th century?
    a) It was the first world map to show America
    b) It was drawn upside down compared to modern maps
    c) It contained instructions for navigating to Atlantis
    d) It was written in a secret code only sailors could read

12. Which famous English explorer attacked Spanish ships and cities in the New World and was later knighted by Queen Elizabeth I?
    a) Sir Francis Bacon
    b) Sir Walter Raleigh
    c) Sir John Hawkins
    d) Sir Francis Drake

13. The Treaty of Tordesillas (1494) divided the newly discovered lands outside Europe between which two countries?
    a) England and France
    b) Portugal and the Netherlands
    c) Spain and Portugal
    d) Spain and the Holy Roman Empire

14. Why did Portuguese explorer Bartolomeu Dias turn back instead of reaching India?
    a) His ships were destroyed in a storm
    b) He was forced to return due to a mutiny
    c) His crew refused to go any farther due to rough waters
    d) He was captured by African tribes along the way

15. Which famous explorer's name is wrongly associated with the discovery of America, despite never setting foot on the continent?
    a) Vasco da Gama
    b) Amerigo Vespucci
    c) Hernán Cortés
    d) James Cook

ANSWERS

1. **a) The Piri Reis Map** – This 16th-century Ottoman map includes detailed depictions of South America and, controversially, what some claim to be Antarctica.

2. **c) Naval warfare with Arab merchants** – Upon reaching India, Vasco da Gama's arrival led to conflict with entrenched Arab trading networks, resulting in violent naval clashes and the beginning of Portuguese dominance in the Indian Ocean.

3. **a) The Vikings had already settled parts of North America centuries earlier** – Columbus' journey was not the first known contact between the Old and New Worlds.

4. **a) El Dorado** – Many European explorers searched in vain for this legendary city of gold.

5. **a) Ibn Battuta** – The Moroccan scholar traveled extensively across Africa, the Middle East, and Asia, documenting his experiences.

6. **b) Portugal** – Portugal's empire included territories in Brazil, Angola, Mozambique, Goa, Malacca, and even Nagasaki. It was the first truly global maritime empire, largely due to its early investments in navigation and trade.

7. **b) To find a westward route to the Spice Islands** – Magellan's voyage aimed to establish a sea route to Asia by sailing westward.

8. **a) Lack of knowledge about ocean currents** – Early explorers struggled to navigate because they didn't fully understand wind and water patterns.

9. **b) It was a great center of trade and scholarship in Africa** – Timbuktu was a major intellectual and commercial hub during the medieval period.

10. **a) Henry Hudson** – His expedition disappeared in the Arctic while searching for a northern sea route to Asia.

11. **b) It was drawn upside down compared to modern maps** – The Fra Mauro Map placed the south at the top, opposite of what is common today.

12. **d) Sir Francis Drake** – Drake was a privateer who circumnavigated the globe and raided Spanish treasure fleets and ports, weakening Spain's control. He was seen as both a hero and a pirate, depending on your side.

13. **c) Spain and Portugal** – The Treaty of Tordesillas, brokered by the Pope, divided the world between Spain (west) and Portugal (east) along a meridian. This led to Brazil falling into Portuguese hands, despite being in South America.

14. **c) His crew refused to go any farther due to rough waters** – Bartolomeu Dias turned back at the Cape of Good Hope due to crew exhaustion and fear.

15. **b) Amerigo Vespucci** – Though the Americas were named after him, he was not the first to "discover" them.

Final Score: How Did You Do?

- 60–75 correct: **Historical Hero**
- 45–59 correct: **Seasoned Scholar**
- 30–44 correct: **Time-Travel Trainee**
- 15–29 correct: **Trivia Tourist**
- 0–14 correct: **Chronologically Confused**

HIDDEN HISTORIES THAT SHAPED THE MODERN WORLD

INDUSTRIAL REVOLUTION – THE STEAM POWERED ERA

The world was changing at a speed no one had ever seen before. Sparks flew, gears turned, and clouds of steam rose as a new era roared to life. In workshops and factories, brilliant minds and bold tinkerers reimagined what was possible, crafting machines that could outwork armies of men and transport dreams across continents. This was the dawn of the industrial age, where once unimaginable inventions began to weave the fabric of the modern world. From smog-filled cities to far-reaching railways, humanity found itself racing headlong into the future.

But not everyone greeted these thundering engines and towering factories with open arms. Beneath the marvels of progress lay stories of struggle, resistance, and the hidden costs of ambition. Some feared the growing machines would devour their way of life, while others dared to dream of harnessing these new powers for the good of all. In this chapter, you'll explore a time of invention and upheaval, curiosity and caution—an era when steam and steel redrew the map of human possibility.

Did you know...?

In Victorian England, people feared being buried alive so much that they invented "safety coffins." These included escape hatches, air tubes, and even bells above ground connected to strings tied to the supposed corpse's hand. Some cemeteries kept a guard on watch, just in case. Though the actual risk was low, stories of premature burial gripped the public imagination—especially in an era obsessed with death, science, and the supernatural.

The Birth of Innovation – How Tech Reshaped the World

The Industrial Revolution brought about an unprecedented wave of technological advancements that transformed everyday life. From awe-inspiring inventions to the rise of mass production, the 19th century marked the birth of the modern world. How much do you know about this era of innovation?

1. Which European city became famous for introducing gas street lighting in 1807, symbolizing the shift toward industrial urban life?
   a) Manchester
   b) London
   c) Paris
   d) Berlin

2. Which invention is often credited with kickstarting the Industrial Revolution?
   a) The steam engine
   b) The telegraph
   c) The internal combustion engine
   d) The typewriter

3. What made the Great Exhibition of 1851 a significant historical event?
   a) It was the first international event dedicated to scientific discoveries
   b) It introduced the world to moving pictures and early cinema
   c) It was the first fair where women were allowed to participate
   d) It hosted the first working telephone demonstration

4. Which revolutionary machine greatly improved textile production in the 18th and 19th centuries?
   a) The Jacquard loom
   b) The cotton gin
   c) The Spinning Jenny
   d) The power loom

5. In which country did the earliest known steam-powered devices originate, long before the Industrial Revolution took hold in Europe?
   A) China
   b) Egypt
   c) Greece
   d) India

6. Which scientist and inventor is credited with developing the first commercially viable steam engine?
   a) James Watt
   b) Thomas Edison
   c) Isambard Kingdom Brunel
   d) Charles Babbage

7. What was the major effect of mechanization on factory workers?
   a) They had to work fewer hours
   b) Many lost their jobs due to automation
   c) They received higher wages due to increased productivity
   d) Factories became safer work environments

8. Which engineering marvel, completed in 1843, was designed by Isambard Kingdom Brunel and revolutionized bridge construction?
   a) The Brooklyn Bridge
   b) The Clifton Suspension Bridge
   c) The Golden Gate Bridge
   d) The Tower Bridge

9. What was the main purpose of the Bessemer process?
   a) To make steam engines more efficient
   b) To mass-produce steel at a lower cost
   c) To develop the first railway system
   d) To create the first electrical power grid

10. What was one of the key reasons why the Industrial Revolution began in Britain?
    a) Britain had an abundance of natural resources like coal and iron
    b) The British government banned all foreign inventions
    c) It was the first country to develop electricity
    d) It had the world's largest population at the time

11. Which transportation innovation drastically improved the movement of goods and people during the Industrial Revolution?
    a) The steam locomotive
    b) The automobile
    c) The hot air balloon
    d) The submarine

12. Who invented the telegraph, which revolutionized long-distance communication?
    a) Alexander Graham Bell
    b) Samuel Morse
    c) Nikola Tesla
    d) Guglielmo Marconi

13. Which material became the backbone of industrialization, allowing for stronger buildings, bridges, and machines?
    a) Bronze
    b) Iron
    c) Steel
    d) Aluminum

14. What was Japan's first major industrial enterprise after opening to the West in the 1850s, inspired by Western models?
a) The Mitsubishi Shipyard
b) The Tomioka Silk Mill
c) The Tokyo Ironworks
d) The Kyoto Textile Guild

15. What was a major consequence of urbanization during the Industrial Revolution?
a) Rural populations increased as people moved away from cities
b) Cities became overcrowded, leading to poor living conditions
c) Factories moved to the countryside to avoid pollution
d) Farming became the dominant industry in Europe

ANSWERS

1. **b) London** – Gas street lighting was introduced in London in 1807 along Pall Mall. It symbolized the modernization of urban life and the growing availability of industrial energy sources for everyday use.

2. **a) The steam engine** – The development of efficient steam engines powered factories, railways, and ships, revolutionizing industry.

3. **a) It was the first international event dedicated to scientific discoveries** – The Great Exhibition brought together inventors and scientists from around the world.

4. **c) The Spinning Jenny** – This device allowed multiple threads to be spun at once, increasing textile production.

5. **c) Greece** – The aeolipile, a primitive steam-powered device, was described by Hero of Alexandria in ancient Greece around the 1st century CE. While it was more of a curiosity than a practical machine, it shows early human interest in steam power.

6. **a) James Watt** – He made key improvements to the steam engine, making it more practical for industrial use.

7. **b) Many lost their jobs due to automation** – Machines replaced many skilled workers, leading to unemployment in some sectors.

8. **b) The Clifton Suspension Bridge** – One of Brunel's most famous projects, this bridge set new engineering standards.

9. **b) To mass-produce steel at a lower cost** – The Bessemer process made steel production cheaper and more efficient, fueling industrial growth.

10. **a) Britain had an abundance of natural resources like coal and iron** – These resources were crucial for powering steam engines and building infrastructure.

11. **a) The steam locomotive** – Railways transformed transportation, making travel and trade faster and more reliable.

12. **b) Samuel Morse** – He developed the Morse code and the telegraph, enabling near-instant communication across great distances.

13. **c) Steel** – Stronger than iron, steel became the key material for construction and machinery.

14. **b) The Tomioka Silk Mill** – Established in 1872, the Tomioka Silk Mill was Japan's first modern factory, representing Japan's industrial transformation during the Meiji Restoration, especially in textile production.

15. **b) Cities became overcrowded, leading to poor living conditions** – As people flocked to industrial cities, housing shortages and sanitation issues worsened.

Rebels Against the Machine

As industrialization spread across Britain in the early 19th century, not everyone welcomed the rise of machines. These struggles echo throughout history, with similar movements resisting technological change even in the modern world.

1. Who were the Luddites, and what was their primary concern?
   a) A radical political group seeking to overthrow the government
   b) Skilled textile workers protesting job losses due to mechanization
   c) Inventors who designed new steam-powered machines
   d) A secret society dedicated to advancing technology

2. Which industry did the Luddites mainly target during their protests?
   a) Coal mining
   b) Shipbuilding
   c) Textile manufacturing
   d) Railway construction

3. What did the Luddites do to resist industrialization?
   a) Organized peaceful protests and strikes
   b) Sent petitions to Parliament demanding higher wages
   c) Smashed machinery and burned factories
   d) Created their own competing factories

4. Who was "General Ludd," the supposed leader of the Luddite movement?
   a) A real military commander who led worker uprisings
   b) A fictional figure, likely inspired by folklore
   c) The British prime minister at the time
   d) An industrialist who sympathized with workers

5. How did the British government respond to the Luddite movement?
   a) By negotiating with workers and improving labor conditions
   b) By executing or imprisoning suspected Luddites
   c) By banning all textile machinery
   d) By offering compensation to displaced workers

6. Which group of rural English laborers destroyed threshing machines during the Swing Riots of 1830, fearing they would lose their livelihoods?
   a) Chartists
   b) Levellers
   c) Swingites
   d) Captain Swing's Men

7. Which late 19th-century Native American religious movement sought to restore traditional ways of life and resist U.S. expansion through communal dancing and spiritual renewal, ultimately leading to the tragic Wounded Knee Massacre?
   a) The Ghost Dance Movement
   b) The Sun Dance Movement
   c) The Longhouse Religion
   d) The Native American Church

8. Why did the Luddites focus on smashing machines rather than attacking factory owners?
   a) They believed machines, not people, were responsible for their suffering
   b) Factory owners had too much military protection
   c) Machines were cheaper to replace than human workers
   d) They wanted to make room for newer, better machines

9. The Mapuche resistance against Chilean and Argentine expansion in the 19th century was partly in response to:
   a) Missionary schools
   b) Industrial railways and land seizures
   c) Mining projects
   d) Livestock taxation

10. Which religious community is well known for rejecting modern technology?
    a) The Mormons
    b) The Amish
    c) The Jesuits
    d) The Druids

11. What 20th-century Peruvian rebel group, founded by university professor Abimael Guzmán, blended Maoist ideology with violent anti-modern rhetoric?
    a) MRTA
    b) Shining Path
    c) Red Sun Collective
    d) Andes Liberation Front

12. What ideology did the Russian revolutionary group "Narodnaya Volya" (People's Will) embrace in the late 1800s, often opposing the urban-industrial future of Russia?
    a) Marxist socialism
    b) Christian monarchism
    c) Agrarian populism
    d) Technocratic futurism

13. The 19th-century "Canut Revolts" in Lyon, France, were led by:
    a) Peasants
    b) Silk weavers opposing mechanization and poor conditions
    c) Factory owners
    d) Railroad workers

14. Which fiction writer famously warned about the dangers of unchecked technological progress?
    a) George Orwell
    b) Isaac Asimov
    c) J.R.R. Tolkien
    d) William Shakespeare

15. What was the primary motivation behind the Amish rejection of modern technology?
    a) Fear of government surveillance
    b) A belief in self-sufficiency and a simple life
    c) A conspiracy theory about machines being cursed
    d) A lack of access to electricity

ANSWERS

1. **b) Skilled textile workers protesting job losses due to mechanization** – The Luddites were mainly concerned that machines would replace skilled labor, leaving them unemployed.

2. **c) Textile manufacturing** – The textile industry was one of the first to experience mechanization, leading to major worker unrest.

3. **c) Smashed machinery and burned factories** – The Luddites resorted to violent tactics to destroy the machines they saw as threats.

4. **b) A fictional figure, likely inspired by folklore** – "General Ludd" was a mythical leader, often invoked to inspire workers.

5. **b) By executing or imprisoning suspected Luddites** – The British government cracked down on the movement harshly, executing several leaders.

6. **d) Captain Swing's Men** – The Swing Riots were a mass rural uprising in England in 1830 where agricultural workers destroyed threshing machines, fearing they would be replaced. Letters were often signed by the fictional "Captain Swing."

7. **b) Ghost Dance Movement** – The Ghost Dance was a spiritual and cultural resistance among Native American tribes, envisioning a world free of white settlers and their railroads, telegraphs, and industrial intrusion.

8. **a) They believed machines, not people, were responsible for their suffering** – Their battle was against technology itself rather than individual factory owners.

9. **b) Industrial railways and land seizures** – The Mapuche resisted industrial developments like railways and agricultural colonization, which threatened their ancestral lands and autonomy in both Chile and Argentina.

10. **b) The Amish** – The Amish reject most modern technology, choosing to live a simple, self-sufficient life.

11. **b) Shining Path** – The Shining Path (Sendero Luminoso) was a brutal Maoist insurgency in Peru in the 1980s–90s, seeking to destroy modern institutions, including those of industrial and capitalist development.

12. **c) Agrarian populism** – Narodnaya Volya believed in a return to communal peasant-based agrarian life, opposing the rise of industrial capitalism in favor of Russia's rural traditions. They famously assassinated Tsar Alexander II.

13. **b) Silk weavers opposing mechanization and poor conditions** – The Canuts were silk weavers in Lyon who revolted multiple times in the 1830s against low wages and mechanized looms, early examples of urban labor rebellion.

14. **a) George Orwell** – Orwell warned about the dangers of surveillance and unchecked technological power in books like *1984*.

15. **b) A belief in self-sufficiency and a simple life** – The Amish resist technology because they believe it disrupts their traditional way of life.

Scientific Oddities – The Bizarre Beliefs of the Past

The 19th century was a time of rapid scientific progress—but it was also a time of strange and sometimes downright absurd beliefs. From misguided medical treatments to bizarre theories about the human mind, many ideas once accepted as fact have since been proven to be nonsense. Let's explore some of the most unusual scientific oddities of the era!

1. Until the late 1800s, what was a common concern among some surgeons about the use of anesthesia?
   a) It could be dangerous or morally questionable
   b) It would slow down surgery
   c) It would make patients forget the experience
   d) It was too expensive to use regularly

2. What was the purpose of phrenology, a pseudoscience popular in the 19th century?
   a) Studying the stars to predict human behavior
   b) Measuring skull shapes to determine personality traits
   c) Using animal magnetism to heal the sick
   d) Analyzing dreams to understand mental illness

3. Which famous astronomer believed in a "hollow Earth" theory and suggested it might be inhabited?
   a) Edmond Halley
   b) Tycho Brahe
   c) Carl Linnaeus
   d) William Herschel

4. Who was the Austrian physician who developed the concept of "animal magnetism," later linked to hypnosis?
   a) Sigmund Freud
   b) Franz Mesmer
   c) Robert Koch
   d) Louis Pasteur

5. Why did doctors in the 19th century prescribe arsenic to patients?
   a) As a painkiller
   b) As a treatment for syphilis and other diseases
   c) To help with digestion
   d) As an early form of chemotherapy

6. What did Victorian-era doctors believe about the human body's four "humors"?
   a) They controlled the patient's mood
   b) They determined intelligence and lifespan
   c) An imbalance of humors caused illness
   d) They influenced the ability to communicate with the dead

7. Which invention helped disprove the miasma theory of disease?
   a) The microscope
   b) The steam engine
   c) The X-ray machine
   d) The stethoscope

8. Which was *not* a dangerous cosmetic product used in the 19th century?
   a) Lead-based face powder
   b) Radium-infused blush
   c) Mercury eyeliner
   d) Formaldehyde lip gloss

9. What unusual experiment did Benjamin Franklin conduct to investigate the transmission of disease?
   a) Swallowing metal filings
   b) Sleeping with a corpse
   c) Sitting in a room filled with "foul air"
   d) Drinking mercury

10. In the early 1800s, some scientists believed that mice and insects could spontaneously generate from:
    a) Rotting meat
    b) Mud mixed with sunlight
    c) Wet hemp cloth
    d) Water and moonlight

11. What was the primary medical purpose of trepanation, an ancient practice that was still occasionally performed in the 19th century?
    a) To relieve pressure on the brain after head injuries or infections
    b) To improve blood circulation
    c) To make people more intelligent
    d) To cure poor vision

12. Which bizarre Victorian medical treatment involved inhaling a very toxic substance?
    a) Smoking arsenic
    b) Mercury vapor therapy
    c) Inhaling carbolic acid
    d) Snuffing radium water

13. Why did people believe in mesmerism, or "animal magnetism"?
    a) They thought magnetic forces in the body could heal disease
    b) It was proven through scientific experiments
    c) It was promoted by Queen Victoria
    d) It was linked to astrology

14. Which 19th-century medical device was originally developed as a treatment for "female hysteria"?
    APPROPRIATE FOR KIDS?
    a) The electric vibrator
    b) The X-ray machine
    c) The iron lung
    d) The hypodermic syringe

15. What led to the eventual rejection of phrenology?
    a) Scientists found no connection between skull shape and intelligence
    b) A major phrenologist admitted it was a fraud
    c) The invention of the MRI proved it wrong
    d) It was banned by the government

ANSWERS

1. **a) It could be dangerous or morally questionable** – Some surgeons and religious leaders worried that anesthesia might harm patients or interfere with the natural or divine order, especially during childbirth. It was even argued that it could sever the link between body and soul.

2. **b) Measuring skull shapes to determine personality traits** – Phrenologists claimed they could tell if someone was a criminal or a genius by feeling the bumps on their head.

3. **a) Edmond Halley** – Yes, of Halley's Comet fame! He suggested Earth had concentric hollow spheres inside, possibly housing life. His theory was used to explain strange compass readings and aurora phenomena.

4. **b) Franz Mesmer** – He believed in "animal magnetism," a mystical force that supposedly influenced health.

5. **b) As a treatment for syphilis and other diseases** – Arsenic was once a common medicine, despite its toxicity.

6. **c) An imbalance of humors caused illness** – This idea dated back to ancient Greece and persisted into the 19th century.

7. **a) The microscope** – It helped scientists discover bacteria, disproving the idea that diseases were caused by bad air.

8. **d) Formaldehyde lip gloss** – Formaldehyde was used in embalming, but not in lip gloss. It became more of a concern in 20th-century beauty products, especially in nail hardeners.

9. **c) Sitting in a room filled with "foul air"** – Before germ theory, people believed in Miasma theory - that diseases like cholera and the plague were caused by foul-smelling air. Franklin reportedly sat in stuffy, stale-smelling rooms to test whether illness followed. He didn't get sick—though the actual transmission of disease would remain mysterious until germ theory was accepted.

10. **c) Wet hemp cloth** – Pre-germ theory, scientists debated spontaneous generation. Some believed that if you left hemp rags in a dark space, they would sprout mice, insects, or even vegetables, seemingly from nowhere.

11. **a) To relieve pressure on the brain after head injuries or infections** – Trepanation involved drilling holes into the skull to relieve pressure and sometimes to "release" spirits.

12. **b) Mercury vapor therapy** – Mercury was used to treat syphilis, but inhaling it often led to poisoning.

13. **a) They thought magnetic forces in the body could heal disease** – Mesmerists believed that invisible energy fields influenced health.

14. **a) The electric vibrator** – It was originally designed to relieve "female hysteria" before becoming a mainstream device.

15. **a) Scientists found no connection between skull shape and intelligence** – Despite its popularity, phrenology was ultimately debunked.

The Hidden Costs of Progress – Pollution and Peril

The Industrial Revolution brought incredible advancements, but it also had a darker side. Cities became overcrowded, factories were dangerous, and pollution created public health disasters. Let's explore some of the strangest and most shocking consequences of rapid industrialization.

1. What was "The Great Stink" of 1858?
   a) A massive fire in London's cheese sector
   b) Too many horses causing an extreme build-up of manure on the streets
   c) A summer where the River Thames smelled so bad it shut down Parliament
   d) A deadly gas leak from a chemical factory

2. What poisonous chemical was commonly used in 19th-century industrial wallpaper, leading to mysterious deaths and green-colored illnesses?
   a) Lead acetate
   b) Arsenic trioxide
   c) Chromium oxide
   d) Mercury nitrate

3. What was a common health hazard for 19th-century matchstick factory workers?
   a) "Match fever" from inhaling toxic fumes
   b) "Phossy jaw," a disease caused by white phosphorus exposure
   c) "Loom lung" from inhaling cotton dust
   d) Lead poisoning from handling metal dyes

4. Why was child labor so common during the Industrial Revolution?
   a) Children were seen as cheap and easily replaceable workers
   b) Many children preferred working to going to school
   c) Factory owners believed children were stronger than adults
   d) The government encouraged child labor to boost the economy

5. What was one of the deadliest effects of coal-burning factories in industrial cities?
   a) Acid rain
   b) The spread of the Black Death
   c) The destruction of farmland
   d) Global cooling

6. What was a major, unintended consequence of the expansion of railroads across colonial Africa in the late 19th and early 20th centuries?
   a) Flooding of native lands
   b) Desertification
   c) Spread of sleeping sickness via tsetse flies
   d) Earthquake-triggered cave-ins

7. What was "Lung Rot," a common disease among coal miners?
   a) A bacterial infection from mine water
   b) Tuberculosis caused by coal dust inhalation
   c) A fungal infection from working in dark tunnels
   d) A lung condition caused by exposure to high-pressure steam

8. Why were women's crinoline skirts considered dangerous in the 19th century?
   a) They could easily catch fire from open flames
   b) The steel hoops often snapped, injuring the wearer
   c) They contained toxic dyes that poisoned the skin
   d) They were so heavy they caused spinal damage

9. Which infamous industrial disaster saw a molasses storage tank burst, flooding part of Boston with a deadly wave?
   a) The Sweet Deluge
   b) The Boston Syrup Spill
   c) The Great Molasses Flood
   d) The Sugar Wave Catastrophe

10. What eerie side-effect was reported by workers in 1800s Scottish flax mills due to exposure to flax dust and humidity?
    a) Skin that glowed in the dark
    b) Hair turning green
    c) Permanent hoarseness
    d) Persistent hallucinations

11. Which industry was known for poisoning workers with mercury, leading to erratic behavior?
    a) Hat-making
    b) Glass-blowing
    c) Coal mining
    d) Textile dyeing

12. What was the main cause of widespread cholera outbreaks in 19th-century cities?
    a) Contaminated drinking water
    b) Air pollution from factories
    c) Overcrowded living conditions
    d) Poor nutrition among factory workers

13. What was a common industrial-era cause of death for young women working in 19th-century textile mills in Britain and the U.S.?
    a) Boiler explosions
    b) Hair caught in machinery
    c) Chemical poisoning
    d) Exhaustion-induced collapse

14. Which law helped reduce child labor by limiting working hours and setting minimum age requirements?
a) The Factory Act of 1833
b) The Poor Law Amendment Act
c) The Education Reform Act
d) The Workhouse Act

15. During the industrial revolution, what was a bizarre but documented social fear among elites about the working classes?
a) That their bodies would adapt to living underground
b) That night shift workers would develop vampire-like habits
c) That they would become addicted to machine noise
d) That exposure to industrial rhythms would make them unfit for democracy

---

ANSWERS

1. **c) A summer where the River Thames smelled so bad it shut down Parliament** – Heat and pollution made the Thames unbearable, forcing lawmakers to address London's sanitation crisis and build an underground sewerage system.

2. **b) Arsenic trioxide** – Victorian wallpaper—especially the fashionable "Scheele's Green"—often contained arsenic, which could turn toxic in damp rooms and cause respiratory illness, neurological issues, and death.

3. **b) "Phossy jaw," a disease caused by white phosphorus exposure** – This condition rotted the jawbones of matchstick workers.

4. **a) Children were seen as cheap and easily replaceable workers** – Factory owners hired children because they could be paid less and fit into small spaces.

5. **a) Acid rain** – Coal-burning released sulfur dioxide, which mixed with rainwater to form acid rain.

6. **c) Spread of sleeping sickness via tsetse flies** – Railroads disrupted ecosystems and helped spread tsetse flies, which carry sleeping sickness (trypanosomiasis). This had devastating effects on both people and livestock, particularly in central and eastern Africa.

7. **b) Tuberculosis caused by coal dust inhalation** – "Lung Rot" was a deadly condition suffered by miners.

8. **a) They could easily catch fire from open flames** – Many women died when their skirts brushed against candles or fireplaces.

9. **c) The Great Molasses Flood** – In 1919, a massive molasses storage tank burst in Boston, sending a wave through the streets that reached speeds of 35 mph and killed 21 people.

10. **c) Permanent hoarseness** – Workers in flax mills developed chronic respiratory problems from inhaling flax dust and working in artificially humidified rooms. Many suffered from permanent hoarseness, and some developed byssinosis, a type of lung disease.

11. **a) Hat-making** – The phrase "mad as a hatter" comes from mercury poisoning among hat-makers.

12. **a) Contaminated drinking water** – Poor sanitation allowed cholera to spread rapidly.

13. **b) Hair caught in machinery** – Many young women and girls worked long hours in textile mills. If their long hair wasn't properly tied or covered, it could get entangled in fast-moving gears, often with fatal or disfiguring results.

14. **a) The Factory Act of 1833** – This law was one of the first major steps in protecting child workers.

15. **d) That exposure to industrial rhythms would make them unfit for democracy** – Some 19th-century elites feared that the monotonous, dehumanizing routines of factory life would create a population too docile or robotic to participate meaningfully in civic life—an early version of today's concerns about automation and alienation.

Railroads and the Race Against Time

The invention of steam-powered railroads transformed societies, shrinking vast distances and revolutionizing industries. But behind the progress lay incredible dangers, harsh labor, and even a few mysteries. Test your knowledge of the age when iron rails reshaped the world!

1. Which country built the first full-scale working railway system?
   a) France
   b) Germany
   c) United Kingdom
   d) United States

2. What was the name of the first full-scale working steam locomotive, built in 1804?
   a) The Rocket
   b) Penydarren locomotive
   c) The Flying Scotsman
   d) Locomotion No. 1

3. How did railroads lead to the invention of time zones?
   a) Trains had trouble running on different local times
   b) Engineers needed precise schedules for fuel efficiency
   c) Countries wanted to track train routes in real-time
   d) Railways relied on astronomical observations

4. What unexpected issue plagued passengers on early steam trains in the 1830s and 1840s?
   a) Cattle stampedes
   b) Flying embers setting clothing alight
   c) Soot-induced nosebleeds
   d) Confusion due to trains reversing mid-journey

5. What was the deadliest railroad disaster of the 19th century?
   a) The Tay Bridge Collapse (1879)
   b) The Great Train Wreck of 1856
   c) The Versailles Rail Accident (1842)
   d) The Ashtabula River Railroad Disaster (1876)

6. Why did Russia build its early railways with a different track gauge than the rest of Europe in the 19th century?
   a) To prevent easy military invasion
   b) A miscalculation by engineers
   c) Frost expansion required wider rails
   d) Imitation of American systems

7. Which famous 19th-century American train line was robbed by Jesse James and his gang in one of the first peacetime train robberies in U.S. history?
   a) The Missouri–Kansas–Texas Railroad
   b) The Union Pacific Railroad
   c) The Chicago, Rock Island and Pacific Railroad
   d) The Atchison, Topeka and Santa Fe Railway

8. Why did railway companies build luxurious "palace cars" in the late 1800s?
   a) To compete with steamships for wealthy travelers
   b) To transport royalty across Europe
   c) To carry important government officials
   d) To reward railway workers with free travel

9. Which legendary "ghost train" is said to appear before disasters?
   a) The Silver Phantom
   b) The St. Louis Ghost Express
   c) The Lincoln Funeral Train
   d) The Phantom of the Rails

10. Which of the following was a direct result of railway development in 19th-century Australia?
    a) Camels being imported for desert transport
    b) Dingo migration across states
    c) Creation of the world's first interstate currency
    d) Official adoption of left-hand driving

11. Which famous railway helped unite the United States by connecting its east and west coasts?
    a) The Transcontinental Railroad
    b) The Great Pacific Railway
    c) The American Iron Line
    d) The Eastern-Western Express

12. Which city's underground railway, the world's first subway system, opened in 1863?
    a) Paris
    b) New York
    c) London
    d) Berlin

13. What was one early criticism of rail travel by Victorian-era doctors and moralists?
    a) It would permanently alter women's reproductive systems
    b) It would cause "railway madness" due to speed
    c) It might break down the concept of personal identity
    d) All of the above

14. Which country built the Trans-Siberian Railway, the longest continuous railway line in the world?
    a) Canada
    b) Russia
    c) China
    d) India

15. Why did some early steam locomotives explode unexpectedly?
    a) Engineers accidentally overloaded the engine
    b) Steam pressure built up too high and burst the boiler
    c) Poorly built tracks caused derailments
    d) Lightning strikes set coal on fire

ANSWERS

1. **c) United Kingdom** – Britain pioneered the first full-scale rail system with the Stockton and Darlington Railway in 1825.

2. **a) Penydarren locomotive** – Built by Richard Trevithick in 1804, the Penydarren locomotive was the first full-scale working steam railway locomotive. Subsequently, the Rocket – designed by George Stephenson in 1829 – proved steam power was the future.

3. **a) Trains had trouble running on different local times** – Before standardized time zones, each town set its own time, making train schedules chaotic.

4. **b) Flying embers setting clothing alight** – Early locomotives often emitted sparks and embers, especially in open carriages. There are records of passengers' hats, dresses, and veils catching fire, leading to changes in carriage design.

5. **c) The Versailles rail accident (1842)** – The accident in France killed more than 200 people when a train derailed and caught fire.

6. **a) To prevent easy military invasion** – Russia intentionally adopted a broader gauge (1,520 mm) than Western Europe, partly to impede enemy trains in case of war—an early example of using infrastructure as a defensive tool.

7. **c) Chicago, Rock Island and Pacific Railroad** – In 1873, Jesse James and his gang robbed a train near Adair, Iowa, marking one of the earliest and most famous train robberies of the Wild West era.

8. **a) To compete with steamships for wealthy travelers** – Rail companies introduced luxurious sleeping and dining cars to attract high-paying passengers.

9. **c) The Lincoln Funeral Train** – Some claim the ghostly image of the train carrying Abraham Lincoln's body can still be seen on its original route.

10. **a) Camels being imported for desert transport** – Australia's rail network couldn't reach all arid regions, so camels (and their Afghan handlers) were brought in to carry freight and supplies to remote outposts, especially before rail lines were fully completed.

11. **a) The Transcontinental Railroad** – Completed in 1869, it revolutionized travel across the U.S.

12. **c) London** – The London Underground opened in 1863, using steam-powered trains.

13. **d) All of the above** – Early rail travel sparked moral panic: some feared the speed would cause mental illness, while others believed women's bodies were too fragile for trains. The idea of "railway madness" was genuinely discussed in the press

14. **b) Russia** – The Trans-Siberian Railway, completed in 1916, stretches over 9,000 km from Moscow to Vladivostok.

15. **b) Steam pressure built up too high and burst the boiler** – Early locomotives lacked safety valves, leading to deadly explosions.

Final Score: How Did You Do?

- 60–75 correct: Historical Hero
- 45–59 correct: Seasoned Scholar
- 30–44 correct: Time-Travel Trainee
- 15–29 correct: Trivia Tourist
- 0–14 correct: Chronologically Confused

WORLD WAR WEIRDNESS & COLD WAR CONSPIRACIES

History isn't always straightforward—sometimes, it takes a turn into the strange, the shadowy, and the downright unbelievable. Welcome to the chapter where truth is often stranger than fiction. Behind the thunder of tanks and the headlines of great battles, there lurked secret plots, bizarre experiments, and cloak-and-dagger operations that seemed pulled straight from the pages of a spy novel. During the chaos of global conflict and the chill of the Cold War, nations scrambled not only for power, but for any advantage, no matter how unlikely or peculiar it seemed.

This is the domain of coded messages and hidden agendas, of mysterious sightings and whispered conspiracies that still fuel curiosity today.

Did you know...?

In 1977, a 72-second radio signal from deep space—known as the "Wow! Signal"—was detected by a telescope in Ohio. It was so unusually strong and precise that astronomer Jerry Ehman wrote "Wow!" in the margin of the printout. Despite decades of analysis, no one has been able to explain its origin. It remains one of the most compelling and mysterious possible signs of extraterrestrial intelligence ever recorded.

Curiosities of the Great War

The First World War was filled with odd inventions, unlikely heroes, and astonishing events that defied expectations. Uncover the strange, the surprising, and the little-known moments that history textbooks often overlook.

1. Of the listed countries, which issued the first war-related propaganda film during WWI?
    a) France
    b) Germany
    c) United Kingdom
    d) United States

2. What unexpected animal was officially used by the British army as an early warning system during WWI?
    a) Cats
    b) Glowworms
    c) Camels
    d) Slugs

3. What major global empire lost more territory than any other as a result of WWI?
    a) Russian Empire
    b) Austro-Hungarian Empire
    c) German Empire
    d) Ottoman Empire

4. What role did Thailand (then Siam) play in WWI?
    a) It remained neutral throughout
    b) It declared war on Germany and Austria-Hungary
    c) It supported Germany as a co-belligerent
    d) It was occupied by British forces

5. What was "The White War" during WWI?
   a) An Arctic naval battle
   b) Italian fighting in the Alps against Austria-Hungary
   c) A code name for chemical warfare
   d) A desert campaign in North Africa

6. Which of these territories saw major combat during WWI?
   a) Brazil
   b) Kenya
   c) Mongolia
   d) Indonesia

7. What strange innovation did the British experiment with in order to breach enemy trenches?
   a) Electrified suits
   b) Armored cows
   c) Portable bridges on wheels
   d) Flame-throwing wheelbarrows

8. Which WWI front involved hand-to-hand combat at altitudes of over 10,000 feet?
   a) Western Front
   b) Mesopotamian Front
   c) Italian Front (Dolomites)
   d) Gallipoli

9. Which of these African colonies was still resisting German control *after* the armistice in 1918?
   a) Togo
   b) Kamerun
   c) German East Africa
   d) South West Africa

10. What was the most common cause of death in the trenches?
    a) Machine gun fire
    b) Artillery
    c) Disease
    d) Gas attacks

11. What happened to the German colony of Qingdao (Tsingtao) in China during WWI?
    a) It was returned to China
    b) It remained German
    c) It was seized by Japan
    d) It became neutral

12. Which rare language did the British Army reportedly use for secure communications in World War I?
    a) Gaelic
    b) Maori
    c) Basque
    d) Zulu

13. Which battle was the deadliest single-day battle for British forces in WWI?
    a) Battle of Ypres
    b) Battle of the Somme
    c) Battle of the Marne
    d) Battle of Passchendaele

14. What effect did WWI have on the use of daylight-saving time?
    a) It was abandoned due to confusion in combat
    b) It was first widely implemented to conserve fuel
    c) It was used only in neutral countries
    d) It was outlawed as unpatriotic

15. What was Gavrilo Princip, the man who triggered WWI, rumored to have been eating when he shot Archduke Franz Ferdinand?
    a) A sandwich
    b) A meat pie
    c) A plum
    d) A bowl of soup

ANSWERS

1. **c) United Kingdom** – The British film *"The Battle of the Somme"* (1916) was one of the first major propaganda films, showing real (and staged) footage to gain public support.

2. **d) Slugs** – Slugs could detect mustard gas faster than humans or traditional sensors, so they were used as early warning systems. Glowworms were used as a natural light source, cats as pest control, and camels for transport in desert campaigns.

3. **d) Ottoman Empire** – The Ottoman Empire collapsed after the war, with its lands divided into mandates and protectorates across the Middle East.

4. **b) It declared war on Germany and Austria-Hungary** – Siam joined the Allies in 1917 to modernize and gain diplomatic recognition.

5. **b) Italian fighting in the Alps against Austria-Hungary** – The "White War" involved brutal combat in the snow-covered Dolomites, including tunneling into glaciers.

6. **b) Kenya** – German and British forces clashed in East Africa, including what is now Kenya, in a long and grueling campaign.

7. **c) Portable bridges on wheels** – These devices were part of experimental trench-crossing equipment, precursors to tank engineering.

8. **c) Italian Front (Dolomites)** – Combat in the Alps included vertical climbs, avalanches, and harsh cold, at elevations over 10,000 feet.

9. **c) German East Africa** – Led by General Paul von Lettow-Vorbeck, German forces resisted until weeks after the European armistice.

10. **b) Artillery** – Though gas and machine guns were feared, **artillery caused the most fatalities** due to its range and destructiveness.

11. **c) It was seized by Japan** – Japan, as an Allied power, took the German-controlled city of Qingdao in 1914, marking its rise in East Asia.

12. **c) Basque** – The British Army is documented to have used Basque speakers to transmit messages during World War I, as the language was little known outside its native region and considered secure for code purposes.

13. **b) Battle of the Somme** – On July 1, 1916, the British suffered nearly 60,000 casualties — the deadliest day in their military history.

14. **b) It was first widely implemented to conserve fuel** – Daylight Saving Time was introduced in Germany and later adopted elsewhere to save energy during the war.

15. **a) A sandwich** – This famous (though possibly apocryphal) story claims Princip was getting a sandwich when the Archduke's car stalled nearby, giving him the chance to strike.

The Strangest Secrets of World War II

World War II was not just a battle of soldiers and machines; it was a war of deception, strange technology, and even bizarre superstitions. From animal weapons to psychic experiments, here are 15 of the most unusual and little-known facts from WWII history.

1. What strange weapon did the British Special Operations Executive (SOE) design using dead animals?
   a) Exploding rats
   b) Poisonous frogs
   c) Radio-controlled cockroaches
   d) Sonic bats

2. What was Operation Mincemeat, one of WWII's most successful deception strategies?
   a) A fake invasion plan planted on a corpse to mislead the Nazis
   b) A campaign to spread food shortages in Germany
   c) A secret plan to smuggle spies inside enemy lines
   d) A psychological warfare tactic involving coded messages in recipes

3. Which ancient relic did the Nazis believe would give them ultimate power if found?
   a) The Ark of the Covenant
   b) The Spear of Destiny
   c) The Philosopher's Stone
   d) The Crown of Charlemagne

4. What type of inflatable military equipment did the Allies use to create fake armies?
   a) Tanks
   b) Warships
   c) Submarines
   d) Fighter jets

5. What unusual animal-based weapon did the U.S. attempt to develop during WWII?
   a) Bat bombs
   b) Parachuting bears
   c) Torpedo sharks
   d) Radio-guided pigeons

6. Why did Hitler believe he was immune to assassination attempts?
   a) He wore a bulletproof vest at all times
   b) He believed he had a supernatural destiny
   c) He had a secret double
   d) His bunker had an advanced air filtration system

7. Which strange Nazi secret project allegedly attempted to create an anti-gravity flying saucer?
   a) The Haunebu Project
   b) The Valkyrie Protocol
   c) The Black Eagle Experiment
   d) The Himmler Initiative

8. What deadly invention did Soviet intelligence use to assassinate targets in exile?
   a) Cyanide-laced cigars
   b) Poisoned bullets and pellets
   c) Radioactive wristwatches
   d) Exploding briefcases

9. How did British intelligence use carrier pigeons during WWII?
   a) To send coded messages from behind enemy lines
   b) As decoys to distract Nazi attack birds
   c) As living bombs fitted with mini-explosives
   d) To detect radio signals in occupied France

10. Which country, despite being officially neutral, was bombed by both the Axis and the Allies during WWII?
    a) Spain
    b) Ireland
    c) Sweden
    d) Switzerland

11. What was the Enigma machine, and why was it so important?
    a) A Nazi code machine that encrypted military communications
    b) A device used by Japan to jam enemy radars
    c) A Soviet weapon that could disrupt enemy radio signals
    d) A chemical formula for an explosive more powerful than TNT

12. What eerie phenomenon was widely reported by pilots during WWII?
    a) Ghost planes with no pilots
    b) Foo fighters—mysterious glowing orbs in the sky
    c) Radio transmissions from the future
    d) Spontaneous disappearances of entire bomber squadrons

13. Why did the Nazis spend resources searching for the lost city of Atlantis?
    a) They believed it held ancient technology
    b) They thought it was the ancestral home of the Aryan race
    c) They wanted to use it as a secret submarine base
    d) They believed its ruins contained an unlimited energy source

14. What was Operation Paperclip?
    a) A secret U.S. program to recruit Nazi scientists after the war
    b) A British mission to steal German war documents
    c) A plan to drop propaganda leaflets over enemy cities
    d) A failed attempt to develop invisible ink for spying

15. Which famous illusionist was recruited by the British military to help with deception tactics?
    a) Jasper Maskelyne
    b) Harry Houdini
    c) David Devant
    d) Jean-Eugène Robert-Houdin

ANSWERS

1. **a) Exploding rats** – The British stuffed dead rats with explosives, hoping German soldiers would throw them into boilers, causing massive explosions.

2. **a) A fake invasion plan planted on a corpse to mislead the Nazis** – The British used a dead body dressed as an officer, with fake invasion plans, to trick the Germans into defending the wrong locations.

3. **b) The Spear of Destiny** – Legend says whoever possesses this spear, allegedly used to pierce Christ's side, would be unbeatable in battle.

4. **a) Tanks** – The "Ghost Army" used inflatable tanks and fake radio chatter to fool the Nazis into thinking massive armies were positioned where they weren't.

5. **a) Bat bombs** – The U.S. developed bombs filled with bats carrying tiny incendiary devices, meant to set enemy buildings on fire.

6. **b) He believed he had a supernatural destiny** – Hitler was deeply superstitious and believed in mystical prophecies that predicted his survival.

7. **a) The Haunebu Project** – Some claim the Nazis worked on a disc-shaped flying craft, though there's no solid evidence it ever existed.

8. **b) Poison-tipped bullets and pellets** – The KGB famously later used a poison-tipped umbrella gun in the Cold War assassination of Bulgarian dissident Georgi Markov.

9. **a) To send coded messages from behind enemy lines** – British intelligence used trained pigeons to carry secret messages between resistance groups and the military.

10. **d) Switzerland** – Despite being neutral, Switzerland was accidentally bombed by both Axis and Allied forces due to navigation errors or misidentification. The Swiss protested vigorously, and the U.S. even paid reparations for certain incidents.

11. **a) A Nazi code machine that encrypted military communications** – The Enigma machine was vital to Nazi communications, but codebreakers at Bletchley Park cracked it, changing the course of the war.

12. **b) Foo fighters—mysterious glowing orbs in the sky** – Pilots from both sides reported seeing strange lights following their planes, but their origin remains unexplained.

13. **b) They thought it was the ancestral home of the Aryan race** – Nazi mystics believed Atlantis was the birthplace of the so-called "master race" and searched for proof.

14. **a) A secret U.S. program to recruit Nazi scientists after the war** – The U.S. secretly brought Nazi scientists, including Wernher von Braun, to work on rocket and space technology.

15. **a) Jasper Maskelyne** – This famous stage magician helped the British military create camouflage and deception tactics, including disguising entire battleships.

The Forgotten Frontiers – Revolutions and Resistance

While World War II is often remembered for the battles in Europe and the Pacific, the conflict also ignited lesser-known struggles across Africa, the Middle East, and Asia. Resistance movements, colonial uprisings, and ideological battles reshaped the global order, setting the stage for decolonization and Cold War rivalries.

1. Which Indian leader allied with Nazi Germany and Imperial Japan in hopes of securing India's independence?
   a) Jawaharlal Nehru
   b) Subhas Chandra Bose
   c) Mahatma Gandhi
   d) Bhagat Singh

2. What was the name of the army Bose formed to fight British rule in India?
   a) The Free India Legion
   b) The Azad Hind Fauj (Indian National Army)
   c) The Bengal Tigers
   d) The Hindustan Brigade

3. Which African resistance movement played a crucial role in helping Allied forces defeat Italian occupation during the East African campaign of World War II?
   a) Mau Mau
   b) Arbegnoch
   c) Mandinka Warriors
   d) Tirailleurs Sénégalais

4. What was the name of the resistance group that fought against Japanese occupation in Vietnam?
   a) Khmer Rouge
   b) Viet Minh
   c) Red Sun Brigade
   d) Indo-Chinese Liberation Army

5. What crucial canal did the Axis powers attempt to seize in North Africa, leading to the Battle of El Alamein?
a) Panama Canal
b) Kiel Canal
c) Suez Canal
d) Corinth Canal

6. Which Southeast Asian nation experienced one of the deadliest Japanese occupations, with an estimated one million civilian deaths?
a) Indonesia
b) Burma (Myanmar)
c) Philippines
d) Malaysia

7. What was the name of the French colonial troops from North and West Africa who fought in WWII?
a) Senegalese Tirailleurs
b) Ashanti Warriors
c) Malian Guards
d) Swahili Strikers

8. Which Middle Eastern country saw a British-Soviet invasion in 1941 to secure its oil fields?
a) Iran
b) Saudi Arabia
c) Iraq
d) Syria

9. Who was the Brazilian leader who joined the Allies in WWII, sending troops to fight in Italy?
a) Getúlio Vargas
b) João Goulart
c) Juscelino Kubitschek
d) Augusto Pinochet

10. Which battle in Burma (Myanmar) was considered a turning point in the fight against Japan?
    a) Battle of Kohima-Imphal
    b) Battle of Saipan
    c) Battle of Midway
    d) Battle of Leyte Gulf

11. Which controversial British wartime policy in 1942 involved confiscating and destroying food stocks and boats in Bengal, contributing to the severity of the 1943 famine?
    a) The Denial Policy
    b) The Quit India Movement
    c) The Royal Navy Strike
    d) The Scorched Earth Policy

12. What was the name of the pro-Axis government installed in China during WWII?
    a) Republic of East China
    b) Wang Jingwei Regime
    c) Greater Asia Confederation
    d) The Kwangtung Protectorate

13. Which African independence leader served in the French army during WWII before leading his country to freedom?
    a) Kwame Nkrumah
    b) Jomo Kenyatta
    c) Léopold Sédar Senghor
    d) Patrice Lumumba

14. What was Japan's strategy in persuading colonial subjects in Asia to support their war effort?
    a) "Asia for the Asians" propaganda
    b) Military scholarships for elite families
    c) Forced conscription and labor camps
    d) Promises of full citizenship in Japan

15. Which major Middle Eastern city was the site of a failed pro-Nazi coup in 1941, leading to British intervention?
    a) Cairo
    b) Baghdad
    c) Damascus
    d) Tehran

ANSWERS

1. **b) Subhas Chandra Bose** – Bose sought military assistance from Axis powers to fight British rule, forming alliances with both Nazi Germany and Japan.

2. **b) The Azad Hind Fauj (Indian National Army)** – Bose led the Indian National Army (INA), which fought alongside Japan in Burma and India.

3. **b) Arbegnoch** – The Arbegnoch, or Ethiopian Patriots, were local resistance fighters who, alongside Allied and Commonwealth forces, helped liberate Ethiopia from Italian occupation during the East African campaign

4. **b) Viet Minh** – Led by Ho Chi Minh, the Viet Minh resisted Japanese occupation and later fought against French colonial rule.

5. **c) Suez Canal** – Control of the Suez Canal was vital for Britain's supply lines, leading to major battles in North Africa.

6. **a) Indonesia** – Japan's brutal occupation of Indonesia resulted in famine, forced labor, and widespread civilian deaths.

7. **a) Senegalese Tirailleurs** – These colonial troops played a key role in the liberation of France, despite facing discrimination.

8. **a) Iran** – Britain and the USSR invaded Iran to secure oil fields and remove a pro-German ruler.

9. **a) Getúlio Vargas** – Brazil joined the war in 1942, sending the "Smoking Snakes" division to fight in Italy.

10. **a) Battle of Kohima-Imphal** – This battle in Burma was a decisive victory against Japan, preventing their advance into India.

11. **a) The Denial Policy** – The British implemented a "denial policy" in Bengal, seizing or destroying rice and boats to prevent their use by the Japanese in case of invasion, which worsened the impact of the Bengal famine.

12. **b) Wang Jingwei Regime** – This puppet government in China collaborated with Japan but was unpopular with the Chinese people.

13. **c) Léopold Sédar Senghor** – Senghor fought for France in WWII before leading Senegal to independence in 1960.

14. **a) "Asia for the Asians" propaganda** – Japan framed its expansion as liberation from Western colonial rule, though in reality, it often replaced European control with its own harsh rule.

15. **b) Baghdad** – In 1941, a pro-Nazi coup in Iraq was crushed by British forces to prevent Axis control in the region.

The Hidden Aftermath of WWII

Though World War II ended in 1945, its consequences reshaped global politics, sparking wars, secret operations, and decolonization struggles that would define the second half of the 20th century. From covert military operations to brutal independence movements, the post-war years were anything but peaceful.

1. Which war, beginning in 1946, marked the first major conflict of the Cold War?
   a) Korean War
   b) First Indochina War
   c) Suez Crisis
   d) Algerian War of Independence

2. Which country remained technically at war with Germany until 1990?
   a) France
   b) Russia
   c) The United Kingdom
   d) The United States

3. Which European country secretly used "stay-behind" paramilitary networks to resist a potential Soviet invasion?
   a) France
   b) Italy
   c) Sweden
   d) Portugal

4. Operation Gladio, NATO's covert Cold War strategy, was *not* involved in political instability in which country?
   a) Portugal
   b) Italy
   c) Greece
   d) Turkey

5. What was the name of the operation that delivered food and supplies to West Berlin after the Soviet blockade?
a) Operation Vittles
b) Operation Rolling Thunder
c) Operation Market Garden
d) Operation Paperclip

6. Which African nation fought a brutal eight-year war for independence from France between 1954 and 1962?
a) Morocco
b) Algeria
c) Tunisia
d) Senegal

7. Which unlikely country offered to take in thousands of Holocaust survivors when many nations refused?
a) Japan
b) Mexico
c) The Dominican Republic
d) South Africa

8. Which Asian country was split into two occupation zones by the U.S. and the Soviet Union after WWII, setting the stage for a later war?
a) Vietnam
b) Korea
c) Japan
d) Taiwan

9. After WWII, what unique currency did the Allied forces issue in Germany to stabilize the economy?
a) Allied Reichsmarks
b) Military Occupation Marks
c) Victory Coupons
d) AM-Lira

10. What was the name of the resistance movement in Kenya against British colonial rule that escalated after WWII?
a) Mau Mau Uprising
b) Zulu Rebellion
c) Kikuyu Revolt
d) Nairobi Wars

11. Which European country experienced a civil war between communist and royalist forces immediately after WWII?
a) Spain
b) Greece
c) Yugoslavia
d) Poland

12. Which WWII agreement set the stage for the Cold War by dividing Europe into Western and Soviet spheres of influence?
a) Treaty of Versailles
b) Yalta Conference
c) Geneva Accords
d) Munich Agreement

13. Which country fought a bitter war against the Dutch after WWII to secure independence?
a) Malaysia
b) Indonesia
c) Philippines
d) Burma

14. Which U.S. policy, announced in 1947, committed America to resisting Soviet expansion worldwide?
a) Marshall Plan
b) Monroe Doctrine
c) Truman Doctrine
d) Eisenhower Plan

15. Which WWII-era event led to a Jewish exodus and violent conflicts in the Middle East after 1948?
    a) The Holocaust
    b) The Balfour Declaration
    c) The Suez Crisis
    d) The Yom Kippur War

ANSWERS

1. **b) First Indochina War** – France's war to maintain control over Vietnam ended in 1954 with their defeat at Dien Bien Phu, leading to U.S. involvement in the region.

2. **d) The United States** – While the Allied powers defeated Nazi Germany in 1945, the U.S. didn't formally end its state of war with Germany until 1990, when German reunification occurred. This technicality was due to legal frameworks surrounding the Allied occupation and Cold War tensions.

3. **b) Italy** – Italy's stay-behind units, part of Operation Gladio, were linked to assassinations and political interference during the Cold War.

4. **d) Portugal** – Under the authoritarian Estado Novo regime until 1974, Portugal was an ally of the West and NATO. However, Gladio's known destabilization efforts were centered on NATO countries facing strong domestic left-wing movements.

5. **a) Operation Vittles** – The Berlin Airlift (1948–1949) supplied food, fuel, and medicine to West Berlin after the Soviets blocked land routes.

6. **b) Algeria** – The Algerian War of Independence was one of the bloodiest decolonization conflicts, ending with Algeria's independence in 1962.

7. **c) The Dominican Republic** – In 1938, dictator Rafael Trujillo offered to take in up to 100,000 Jewish refugees, though fewer than 1,000 ultimately arrived. This was one of the few open offers of refuge for Jews before and after the war, as many countries closed their borders or imposed quotas.

8. **b) Korea** – The division of Korea led to the Korean War (1950–1953), which permanently split the country into North and South.

9. **b) Military Occupation Marks** – To stabilize the economy and avoid the chaos of the Weimar hyperinflation era, the Allies introduced the Allied Military Currency (AMC), also known as Occupation Marks, to be used in occupied Germany. These helped re-establish economic control and prevent a currency vacuum after the Nazi regime collapsed.

10. **a) Mau Mau Uprising** – The rebellion against British rule in Kenya (1952–1960) led to mass detentions and brutal counterinsurgency tactics.

11. **b) Greece** – The Greek Civil War (1946–1949) was one of the first Cold War conflicts, with U.S. and British backing for the royalist government against communist forces.

12. **b) Yalta Conference** – The 1945 Yalta agreement divided Europe, setting the stage for Cold War tensions.

13. **b) Indonesia** – Indonesia's independence struggle against Dutch forces lasted from 1945 to 1949, ending in a hard-fought victory.

14. **c) Truman Doctrine** – Announced in 1947, it committed the U.S. to countering Soviet influence worldwide, leading to interventions in Korea and Vietnam.

15. **a) The Holocaust** – The trauma of the Holocaust (alongside factors such as the end of the British Mandate and regional politics) led to the establishment of Israel in 1948, triggering conflicts with Arab nations and ongoing regional tensions.

Beyond the Cuban Missile Crisis

Though the Cuban Missile Crisis in 1962 is often seen as the most dramatic moment of the Cold War, its effects rippled far beyond Cuba and the United States. The global struggle between the U.S. and the Soviet Union shaped revolutions, coups, and independence movements from Latin America to Africa, leaving behind a legacy of conflict and intervention that still influences world politics today.

1. Which Latin American country became the first to undergo a successful socialist revolution during the Cold War?
    a) Chile
    b) Venezuela
    c) Cuba
    d) Nicaragua

2. Where did the U.S. Navy secretly place surveillance devices to tap Soviet communications during the Cold War?
    a) On the hulls of Soviet ships
    b) In undersea telephone cables
    c) Inside Arctic ice stations
    d) In abandoned oil platforms

3. Which Central American country saw its government overthrown in a 1954 CIA-led coup, largely to protect U.S. corporate interests?
    a) El Salvador
    b) Guatemala
    c) Costa Rica
    d) Honduras

4. 1. What bizarre object did the CIA use to try to spy on the Soviets during the 1960s?
    a) A robotic pigeon
    b) A cat fitted with a microphone
    c) A fake sewer grate with a camera
    d) A remote controlled spider

5. In which African country did both the CIA and the KGB back opposing sides during the Cold War, turning a civil war into a proxy conflict?
a) Algeria
b) Angola
c) Ethiopia
d) Sudan

6. Which leader of Chile was overthrown in a U.S.-backed coup on September 11, 1973?
a) Augusto Pinochet
b) Salvador Allende
c) Juan Perón
d) Hugo Chávez

7. In 1962, which country came dangerously close to nuclear war with the United States due to a misunderstanding in a submarine?
a) Cuba
b) Soviet Union
c) China
d) North Korea

8. What event in 1983 led the U.S. to invade the small Caribbean island of Grenada?
a) A Soviet missile base was discovered
b) A Marxist government took power and aligned with Cuba
c) The country declared war on the U.S.
d) Fidel Castro personally led a rebellion there

9. Which Cold War-era leader was famously overthrown and executed in Romania in 1989?
a) Slobodan Milošević
b) Nicolae Ceaușescu
c) Josip Broz Tito
d) Erich Honecker

10. What strange method did the East German Stasi allegedly use to track dissidents?
    a) Scent samples collected from chairs
    b) Remote-controlled bees with microphones
    c) Dusting newspapers with glowing powder
    d) Voice recognition from typewriters

11. Which U.S. president initiated the Iran-Contra scandal, illegally funding Nicaraguan rebels with profits from arms sales to Iran?
    a) Jimmy Carter
    b) Ronald Reagan
    c) Richard Nixon
    d) George H.W. Bush

12. Which 1961 failed U.S.-backed invasion attempted to overthrow Fidel Castro in Cuba?
    a) Operation Mongoose
    b) The Bay of Pigs invasion
    c) The Cuban Missile Crisis
    d) The Havana Uprising

13. Which Asian country fought a long war against the U.S. and its allies, only to emerge as a communist state in 1975?
    a) Cambodia
    b) Laos
    c) Vietnam
    d) South Korea

14. Which country accidentally almost started WWIII by mistaking a research rocket for a nuclear missile in 1995?
    a) United States
    b) Russia
    c) China
    d) North Korea

15. What Cold War project involved the U.S. launching a massive number of tiny metal needles into Earth's orbit?
    a) Project Polaris
    b) Operation Space Web
    c) Project West Ford
    d) Operation Eyesky

ANSWERS

1. **c) Cuba** – The Cuban Revolution (1959) led by Fidel Castro made Cuba a Soviet ally and a major Cold War flashpoint.

2. **b) In undersea telephone cables** – The U.S. Navy, through missions like Operation Ivy Bells, placed wiretaps on Soviet undersea communication cables to gather intelligence during the Cold War. They also designed a fake whale submarine to secretly deploy underwater surveillance near Soviet waters. The disguise helped it avoid detection from both radar and sonar.

3. **b) Guatemala** – The U.S. overthrew Jacobo Árbenz in 1954 to protect the interests of the United Fruit Company, setting a precedent for Cold War interventions.

4. **b) A cat fitted with a microphone** – The CIA's "Acoustic Kitty" project attempted to surgically implant listening devices into cats to spy on Soviet officials. The project failed dramatically when the first cat was run over by a taxi shortly after being released.

5. **b) Angola** – In Angola's civil war (1975–2002), the U.S. and South Africa supported one faction (UNITA), while the USSR and Cuba supported the other (MPLA). It became one of the most intense Cold War proxy wars in Africa.

6. **b) Salvador Allende** – Chile's socialist president was ousted in a U.S.-backed coup, leading to Pinochet's dictatorship.

7. **b) Soviet Union** – During the Cuban Missile Crisis, a Soviet submarine (B-59) was depth-charged by U.S. ships. The crew believed war had begun and nearly launched a nuclear torpedo, but Vasily Arkhipov, one officer, refused to authorize it — possibly preventing WWIII.

8. **b) A Marxist government took power and aligned with Cuba** – The U.S. invaded Grenada in 1983 to prevent a pro-communist regime from solidifying ties with the USSR.

9. **b) Nicolae Ceaușescu** – Romania's brutal communist dictator was overthrown and executed as part of the revolutions that swept Eastern Europe in 1989.

10. **a) Scent samples collected from chairs** – The East German Stasi collected scent samples by making suspects sit on special cloths. Dogs were later used to track these scents — an incredibly odd yet real surveillance tactic.

11. **b) Ronald Reagan** – The Iran-Contra scandal exposed illegal U.S. arms sales to Iran, with profits funding anti-communist rebels in Nicaragua.

12. **b) The Bay of Pigs invasion** – The U.S.-backed Cuban exiles failed to overthrow Fidel Castro in 1961, strengthening his position.

13. **c) Vietnam** – The Vietnam War ended in 1975 with a communist victory, marking one of the U.S.'s biggest Cold War defeats.

14. **b) Russia** – In 1995, Norway launched a scientific rocket to study the northern lights, but Russia briefly mistook it for a U.S. nuclear missile, almost triggering a retaliatory strike. President Boris Yeltsin even activated his nuclear briefcase before the confusion was resolved.

15. **c) Project West Ford** – The U.S. launched 480 million copper needles into orbit in Project West Ford to create an artificial ionosphere in case the Soviets cut communication. It created a short-lived but controversial metal belt around Earth.

Final Score: How Did You Do?

- 60–75 correct: Historical Hero
- 45–59 correct: Seasoned Scholar
- 30–44 correct: Time-Travel Trainee
- 15–29 correct: Trivia Tourist
- 0–14 correct: Chronologically Confused

MODERN MAYHEM & 20TH CENTURY TWISTS

POP CULTURE & POLITICAL PUZZLES

The final decades of the 20th century were a whirlwind of revolutions—not just in politics and technology, but in culture, memory, and imagination. From flickering television screens to global youth movements, new ideas and influences swept across borders with unprecedented speed. Films reimagined history for the big screen, sometimes bending facts in the name of spectacle. Meanwhile, music turned up the volume on rebellion, giving voice to generations eager to challenge the status quo. In every corner of life, creativity collided with controversy, and history itself often felt like it was being rewritten in real time.

Yet beneath the bright lights and loud anthems, deeper puzzles unfolded. Collective memories seemed to shift in strange ways, old empires crumbled, and predictions of the future—both wild and strangely accurate—kept people guessing at what tomorrow might bring.

Did you know...?

In 1969, while millions watched the Moon landing, a man in Paraguay legally declared himself "President of the World" and issued passports to "citizens of Earth." In fact, the 20th century saw a rise in self-declared micronations and eccentric "sovereign" rulers, from floating sea forts to backyard kingdoms. It was a time of both serious political upheaval and deeply imaginative resistance to conventional authority.

Strange & Surprising Stories in Modern History

The postwar 20th century was a time of rapid change and global redefinition. From the Cold War and civil rights movements to pop culture revolutions and political upheaval, the decades after World War II were anything but quiet. Get ready to test your knowledge of the people, events, and ideas that shaped the modern world!

1. Which country was briefly ruled by a pirate radio DJ in the 1960s?
   a) Liechtenstein
   b) Malta
   c) The Principality of Sealand
   d) Iceland

2. What was the *Green Revolution* in the 1950s–70s?
   a) An environmental protest movement in the USA
   b) A nuclear disarmament campaign
   c) A series of agricultural innovations increasing global food production
   d) A Marxist movement in Latin America

3. In 1960, which African nation gained independence and then saw 17 changes of government in just a year?
   a) Nigeria
   b) Democratic Republic of Congo
   c) Senegal
   d) Ghana

4. What was the "Great Smog" of London in 1952 caused by?
   a) A volcanic eruption
   b) Exhaust fumes from newly widespread cars
   c) A mix of weather conditions and coal smoke
   d) An industrial chemical leak

5. What unexpected fashion item was inspired by post-war rationing of nylon?
   a) Plastic raincoats
   b) Painted-on stockings
   c) PVC corsets
   d) Paper dresses

6. Which country detonated a nuclear bomb under a desert in the 1970s to create an artificial lake?
   a) India
   b) USA
   c) Soviet Union
   d) China

7. In which country did a revolution start due to the banning of music concerts in the 1980s?
   a) East Germany
   b) Yugoslavia
   c) Romania
   d) Estonia

8. Why did the Netherlands have to import thousands of bicycles in 1945?
   a) Their bikes had been stolen by retreating Nazis
   b) A flood destroyed major cities and roads
   c) Bicycle factories were bombed
   d) A new fuel shortage boosted bike demand

9. In 1974, a lone Japanese soldier was discovered still fighting WWII in which country?
   a) Guam
   b) Malaysia
   c) Philippines
   d) Papua New Guinea

10. Which African nation planned and built a new, centrally located capital city to ease ethnic tensions after independence?
    a) Ghana
    b) Nigeria
    c) Tanzania
    d) Ivory Coast

11. What was "Operation Ajax" in 1953?
    a) A Dutch clean-up mission after flooding
    b) A British plan to test chemical weapons
    c) A CIA coup to remove Iran's Prime Minister
    d) A failed rocket launch by West Germany

12. Which Asian nation switched its entire road system from left-hand to right-hand driving overnight in 1967?
    a) Thailand
    b) Japan
    c) Pakistan
    d) Sweden

13. What was the "Mau Mau Uprising"?
    a) A Maoist rebellion in China
    b) A Kenyan revolt against British colonial rule
    c) A conflict over fishing rights in the Pacific
    d) A radical student movement in Singapore

14. What unusual event happened in Iceland in 1975, drawing attention to gender equality?
    a) All female workers went on strike for a day
    b) Parliament became 70% female
    c) Women burned bras in the streets
    d) The President stepped down for a woman VP

15. What was "The Great Emu War" in Australia?
    a) A government campaign to cull emus with military force
    b) A satirical play mocking British rule
    c) A protest over endangered species laws
    d) A failed attempt to breed giant emus for meat export

ANSWERS

1. **c) The Principality of Sealand** – A WWII sea fort off the UK coast was declared a "micronation" in 1967 by a pirate radio DJ.

2. **c) A series of agricultural innovations increasing global food production** – The Green Revolution introduced high-yield crops and fertilizers, especially in India and Mexico.

3. **b) Democratic Republic of Congo** – After independence from Belgium in 1960, Congo plunged into chaos, coups, and secessions.

4. **c) A mix of weather conditions and coal smoke** – The Great Smog killed an estimated 12,000 people in London due to coal smoke trapped by weather.

5. **b) Painted-on stockings** – With nylon rationed, women would draw "seams" on their legs to simulate stockings.

6. **c) Soviet Union** – The Soviets detonated nuclear bombs in remote Kazakhstan to create lakes and craters as part of peaceful nuclear explosion experiments.

7. **d) Estonia** – The 1987 "Singing Revolution" in Estonia was sparked by protests over bans on cultural expression, including music.

8. **a) Their bikes had been stolen by retreating Nazis** – German forces took Dutch bikes during their retreat, leaving the population without basic transport.

9. **c) Philippines** – Hiroo Onoda surrendered in 1974 after hiding in the jungle for nearly 30 years, unaware the war had ended.

10. **b) Nigeria** – Nigeria created Abuja as a neutral, centrally located capital. Independence came in 1960. The new city was planned and built in the late 1970s and officially became the capital in 1991.

11. **c) A CIA coup to remove Iran's Prime Minister** – Operation Ajax overthrew Mohammad Mossadegh and reinstated the Shah, a key event in modern Iranian history.

12. **d) Sweden** – Known as "Dagen H," Sweden changed driving sides on September 3, 1967, in a highly coordinated effort.

13. **b) A Kenyan revolt against British colonial rule** – The Mau Mau Uprising (1952–1960) was a major anti-colonial insurgency.

14. **a) All female workers went on strike for a day** – 90% of Icelandic women stopped work on October 24, 1975, demanding equal pay and rights.

15. **a) A government campaign to cull emus with military force** – In 1932, Australia's army failed to reduce emu numbers with machine guns, in what became known as the "Emu War."

Hollywood vs. History – Dubious "Historical" Movies

Hollywood loves a good historical epic, but accuracy often takes a backseat to drama, action, and entertainment. While some films aim for authenticity, many twist facts, exaggerate characters, or outright invent events to create a more compelling story.

1. In *Braveheart* (1995), what historically inaccurate outfit does Mel Gibson's William Wallace famously wear?
   a) Chainmail
   b) A blue toga
   c) A kilt and face paint
   d) A Roman tunic

2. Which major historical figure in *Gladiator* (2000) was inaccurately portrayed as dying in the Colosseum?
   a) Julius Caesar
   b) Emperor Commodus
   c) Marcus Aurelius
   d) Caligula

3. What crucial detail about Pocahontas did Disney's *Pocahontas* (1995) get completely wrong?
   a) She never met John Smith
   b) She was actually a warrior
   c) She and John Smith were never romantically involved
   d) She lived her entire life in America

4. Why was *U-571* (2000) controversial in the UK?
   a) It falsely credited Americans for a British naval success
   b) It depicted Winston Churchill as incompetent
   c) It showed the British surrendering to the Germans
   d) It ignored the role of the Royal Air Force

5. In *The Last Samurai* (2003), what is inaccurate about Tom Cruise's character's role in Japan?
   a) There was no American samurai
   b) The samurai never fought against modernization
   c) The real last samurai was Korean
   d) The character was based on a Russian soldier

6. What major historical event does *The Patriot* (2000) misrepresent?
   a) The Battle of Waterloo
   b) The American Revolution
   c) The French Revolution
   d) The War of 1812

7. What famous shipwreck film added an entirely fictional romance that never happened?
   a) *Master and Commander*
   b) *Titanic*
   c) *Pearl Harbor*
   d) *The Bounty*

8. In *300* (2006), how many Spartans actually fought at the Battle of Thermopylae?
   a) 300
   b) 7,000
   c) 10,000
   d) 100

9. Which historical ruler was turned into an over-the-top supervillain in *Alexander* (2004)?
   a) Genghis Khan
   b) Napoleon Bonaparte
   c) King Darius III
   d) Julius Caesar

10. What historical error does *Pearl Harbor* (2001) make about the attack?
    a) Japan bombed Los Angeles
    b) The U.S. immediately launched a counterattack
    c) The main characters are involved in the Doolittle Raid, which happened months later
    d) Hawaii was a U.S. state at the time

11. Which of these is *not a reason that* historians criticize *Apocalypto* (2006) for its depiction of the Mayan civilization?
    a) The actors spoke an invented language rather than Mayan
    b) The timeline of the Spanish arrival is wrong
    c) It mixes Aztec and Mayan cultures
    d) It inaccurately portrayed them as brutal, bloodthirsty killers

12. In *Robin Hood* (2010), what historical mistake does the film make about King John?
    a) He was actually well-liked
    b) He won the war against France
    c) He died before signing the Magna Carta
    d) He was a Viking

13. What famous historical battle in *Troy* (2004) ignores the decade-long war and condenses it into a few days?
    a) Battle of Marathon
    b) Battle of Hastings
    c) The Trojan War
    d) The Battle of Actium

14. In *Braveheart*, which historical character's love affair is completely impossible?
    a) William Wallace and Queen Isabella
    b) Robert the Bruce and Joan of Arc
    c) Edward II and Joan of Arc
    d) Henry V and Isabella of Spain

15. Which Roman emperor was unfairly demonized in *Gladiator*, despite being more complex in reality?
    a) Nero
    b) Caligula
    c) Commodus
    d) Tiberius

ANSWERS

1. **c) A kilt and face paint** – Kilts weren't worn in Wallace's time, and the blue face paint was from an era 1,000 years earlier.

2. **b) Emperor Commodus** – He was actually strangled in his bath by a wrestler, not killed in a dramatic Colosseum battle.

3. **c) She and John Smith were never romantically involved** – Pocahontas was around 10 years old when she met Smith, and she later married John Rolfe.

4. **a) It falsely credited Americans for a British naval success** – The British actually captured the German Enigma machine, but *U-571* gave credit to the Americans, angering UK audiences.

5. **a) There was no American samurai** – The film's hero is loosely based on a French military advisor, not an American soldier.

6. **b) The American Revolution** – *The Patriot* inaccurately depicted the British as brutal war criminals, including a massacre that never happened.

7. **b) *Titanic*** – The love story between Jack and Rose was completely fictional.

8. **b) 7,000** – While 300 Spartans were famous for holding the pass, they were backed by thousands of other Greek troops.

9. **c) King Darius III** – The Persian king was portrayed as a coward, despite being a formidable ruler who fought Alexander the Great.

10. **c) The main characters are involved in the Doolittle Raid, which happened months later** – The raid on Tokyo was in April 1942, long after the attack on Pearl Harbor.

11. **a) The actors spoke an invented language rather than Mayan** – The film did use the Yucatec Maya language, although it is a modern Maya language, not Classical Mayan.

12. **c) He died before signing the Magna Carta** – King John signed the Magna Carta in 1215 but later ignored it. The film wrongly suggests he was deposed immediately.

13. **c) The Trojan War** – The war lasted about 10 years, but the movie condenses it into a few days.

14. **a) William Wallace and Queen Isabella** – She was a child in France when Wallace was executed.

15. **c) Commodus** – He was cruel but ruled for over a decade, not the incompetent maniac depicted in *Gladiator*.

The Power of Music and Youth Culture

Throughout history, music and art have been driving forces behind youth movements, inspiring rebellion, shaping subcultures, and sometimes even inciting moral panic. From the early days of rock 'n' roll to the rise of hip hop and the digital revolution, young people have used music as a way to express identity, challenge authority, and push cultural boundaries.

1. What famous 1950s musician was condemned for his dance moves, which were seen as too provocative for young audiences?
   a) Chuck Berry
   b) Buddy Holly
   c) Elvis Presley
   d) Little Richard

2. What countercultural trend in 1950s France emphasized boredom, irony, and urban wandering?
   a) Nouvelle Vague
   b) Lettrism
   c) Situationism
   d) Dada

3. What protest song became an anthem of the Civil Rights Movement and was even feared by authorities?
   a) "We Shall Overcome"
   b) "Blowin' in the Wind"
   c) "Say It Loud – I'm Black and I'm Proud"
   d) "People Get Ready"

4. The "Third Cinema" movement, which began in Latin America in the 1960s, was meant to:
   a) Celebrate Hollywood-style glamour
   b) Document indigenous myths
   c) Create revolutionary cinema opposed to both Hollywood and Soviet models
   d) Promote educational children's films

5. The 1968 global protest movements were sparked by unrest in:
   a) Canada and the UK
   b) China and India
   c) France, Mexico, and the U.S.
   d) Brazil and the Netherlands

6. The Bauhaus influence on postwar design and art schools re-emerged in the 1960s in what way?
   a) Through folk revivalism
   b) In anti-modernist sculpture
   c) As modular, socially conscious design and community art practice
   d) In military-themed industrial design

7. What musician's music videos were so controversial in the 1980s that some were banned from television?
   a) Cyndi Lauper
   b) Michael Jackson
   c) Madonna
   d) Prince

8. What was the "Satanic Panic" of the 1980s, and how did it affect perceptions of heavy metal music?
   a) Fans demanded Satanic music on the radio
   b) Schools banned country music
   c) Metal bands were accused of promoting Satanism
   d) A religious music trend began

9. Why was the song "Strange Fruit" by Billie Holiday particularly controversial when revived in the civil rights era?
   a) It depicted lynching in graphic terms
   b) It encouraged alcohol use
   c) It plagiarized a church hymn
   d) It mocked the national anthem

10. What is the term for cultural blending resulting from global exchange post-WWII, particularly in music and fashion?
    a) Cultural monolithism
    b) Hyper-nationalism
    c) Syncretism
    d) Feudalism

11. Which 1960s Japanese art movement used destructive performance to protest postwar conformity and consumerism?
    a) Gutai Group
    b) Mono-ha
    c) Superflat
    d) Kaizen

12. Why did some politicians call for rap music to be censored in the 1990s?
    a) They believed it encouraged religious extremism
    b) They feared it supported anarchy
    c) They accused it of promoting violence and misogyny
    d) They claimed it was un-American

13. What cultural legacy did the 1977 New York City blackout unexpectedly leave?
    a) A boom in avant-garde theatre
    b) A wave of looting that helped seed the birth of hip-hop, as looted turntables and sound systems became tools for DJs
    c) Riots that banned large concerts in the city for a decade
    d) The sudden popularity of unplugged acoustic albums

14. What global music movement in the 2010s used streaming and social media to break cultural barriers?
    a) EDM underground
    b) Jazz-funk revival
    c) K-pop and reggaeton
    d) Indie folk explosion

15. Which African nation became a hub of artistic experimentation in the 1960s following independence, known for its avant-garde cinema and jazz scene?
    a) Nigeria
    b) Ghana
    c) Senegal
    d) Ethiopia

ANSWERS

1. **c) Elvis Presley** – His provocative dance moves sparked national controversy, symbolizing youth rebellion and challenging cultural norms.

2. **c) Situationism** – Founded by Guy Debord, it promoted "psychogeography" and critiques of capitalist spectacle through art.

3. **a) "We Shall Overcome"** – A peaceful but powerful anthem of the Civil Rights Movement, it frightened authorities because of its unifying message.

4. **c) Create revolutionary cinema opposed to both Hollywood and Soviet models** – Third Cinema critiqued both capitalist and authoritarian narratives in favor of revolutionary, grassroots stories.

5. **c) France, Mexico, and the U.S.** – 1968 saw student protests, worker strikes, and civil rights uprisings in multiple countries simultaneously.

6. **c) As modular, socially conscious design and community art practice** – Bauhaus ideals merged with activist and ecological design in schools and collectives.

7. **c) Madonna** – Videos like *Like a Prayer* used religious and sexual imagery, causing backlash and bans.

8. **c) Metal bands were accused of promoting Satanism** – The Satanic Panic led to unfounded claims that bands like Slayer were embedding evil messages.

9. **a) Strange Fruit** – Written by a communist poet, "Strange Fruit" was an eerie, poetic indictment of lynching and racism, suppressed for decades.

10. **c) Syncretism** – Cultures blended elements in new ways due to migration, media, and youth culture.

11. **a) The Gutai Group** – This movement embraced chaos, destruction, and unconventional materials to rebel against traditional art forms.

12. **c) They accused it of promoting violence and misogyny** – Critics used this argument to push for rap censorship, igniting debates about artistic freedom.

13. **b) A wave of looting** – During the blackout, looted DJ gear helped launch what became hip-hop.

14. **c) K-pop and reggaeton** – Artists like BTS and Bad Bunny used streaming and social media to build global fanbases across language and culture barriers.

15. **c) Senegal** – Under leader Léopold Senghor artistic expression tied to postcolonial identity was actively encouraged.

Soviet Union Falls – The World's Most Unexpected Breakup

For nearly half a century, the Soviet Union was one of the two superpowers dominating global politics, armed with nuclear weapons and a vast sphere of influence. But in just a few short years, this seemingly indestructible empire crumbled, leading to the end of the Cold War and reshaping the world forever. How did it all happen so quickly, and what were the unexpected factors behind one of the most dramatic political collapses in history?

1. In what year did the Soviet Union officially dissolve, marking the end of the Cold War?
    a) 1989
    b) 1991
    c) 1993
    d) 1995

2. What Soviet leader's policies of *glasnost* (openness) and *perestroika* (restructuring) unintentionally sped up the collapse of the USSR?
    a) Leonid Brezhnev
    b) Nikita Khrushchev
    c) Mikhail Gorbachev
    d) Joseph Stalin

3. What was the significance of the 1989 "Baltic Way"?
    a) A smuggling route used to escape the USSR
    b) A mass human chain across three countries demanding independence
    c) A military parade that turned into a riot
    d) A secret KGB tunnel between Baltic capitals

4. Which popular Western product became so desirable in the USSR that it was used as informal currency in some places during the 1980s?
   a) Levi's jeans
   b) Coca-Cola
   c) Sony Walkmans
   d) Marlboro cigarettes

5. What major nuclear disaster in 1986 exposed the Soviet Union's inability to handle crises and severely damaged its credibility?
   a) The Three Mile Island accident
   b) The Fukushima disaster
   c) The Chernobyl explosion
   d) The Mayak explosion

6. What was the "August Coup" of 1991?
   a) A bloodless military takeover by a reformist general
   b) A failed attempt by hardliners to seize power from Gorbachev
   c) A diplomatic rebellion led by the Baltic states
   d) An attempt by Chechnya to launch a pre-emptive nuclear strike

7. Which group of individuals became extremely wealthy by acquiring former Soviet industries in the 1990s?
   a) The Red Army generals
   b) The Soviet elite
   c) Russian oligarchs
   d) Communist Party members

8. Which Soviet republic was the first to declare independence, sparking the breakup of the USSR?
   a) Ukraine
   b) Estonia
   c) Lithuania
   d) Belarus

9. What economic crisis in the late 1980s and early 1990s led to extreme shortages of food and basic goods across the Soviet Union?
   a) The Great Depression
   b) The Oil Price Collapse
   c) The Soviet Famine
   d) The Ruble Crisis

10. In a final symbolic moment in December 1991, what happened just after Gorbachev resigned on live television?
    a) He was arrested
    b) The Soviet flag was lowered for the last time over the Kremlin
    c) The U.S. ambassador declared victory
    d) His resignation speech was cut off by a rerun of "Swan Lake"

11. What agreement, signed in December 1991, formally ended the Soviet Union and established the Commonwealth of Independent States (CIS)?
    a) The Helsinki Accords
    b) The Minsk Agreement
    c) The Belavezha Accords
    d) The Warsaw Pact

12. What happened to the vast Soviet nuclear arsenal after the USSR collapsed?
    a) The U.S. took control of all Soviet nuclear weapons
    b) It remained entirely in Russian hands
    c) Some weapons were left in former Soviet republics, creating security concerns
    d) All nuclear weapons were immediately dismantled

13. How did Boris Yeltsin gain worldwide fame during the 1991 coup attempt?
    a) He led an armed rebellion against the military
    b) He fled to the U.S. and sought asylum
    c) He stood on a tank and publicly defied the coup leaders
    d) He negotiated a peaceful transition of power

14. What peculiar border-related event occurred during the Soviet collapse involving the village of Baarle?
    a) It was claimed by four different countries
    b) Its residents elected their own mini-republic
    c) It became an ungoverned "free town" with no official state
    d) It had a confusing checkerboard pattern of land ownership at the border

15. How has the fall of the Soviet Union shaped modern conflicts in former Soviet states like Ukraine and Georgia?
    a) It had no lasting impact
    b) It led to ongoing tensions and conflicts over borders and political influence
    c) The breakup resulted in complete peace in the region
    d) The former Soviet states all quickly became stable democracies

---

ANSWERS

1. **b) 1991** – The Soviet Union officially dissolved on December 26, 1991, marking the end of the Cold War.

2. **c) Mikhail Gorbachev** – His policies of openness (*glasnost*) and restructuring (*perestroika*) unintentionally accelerated the Soviet collapse.

3. **b) A mass human chain across three countries demanding independence** – On August 23, 1989, approximately 2 million people formed a 600 km human chain across Estonia, Latvia, and Lithuania, in a peaceful protest against Soviet occupation. It was a striking display of unity and nonviolent resistance.

4. **a) Levi's jeans** – In the USSR, Levi's jeans were seen as status symbols of the West and could be traded informally on the black market. They became tokens of rebellion, modernity, and freedom.

5. **c) The Chernobyl explosion** – This nuclear disaster exposed deep flaws in Soviet governance and secrecy.

6. **b) A failed attempt by hardliners to seize power from Gorbachev** – In August 1991, members of the Soviet government attempted a coup to halt reforms and prevent the USSR's collapse. It failed, but fatally weakened the Union's remaining cohesion.

7. **c) Russian oligarchs** – These businessmen took control of state industries, becoming extremely wealthy.

8. **c) Lithuania** – It was the first republic to formally declare independence in March 1990. Estonia was the first to declare "sovereignty" within the USSR in 1988, but Lithuania was the first to declare full independence.

9. **d) The Ruble Crisis** – Economic mismanagement led to hyperinflation and shortages.

10. **b) The Soviet flag was lowered for the last time over the Kremlin** – On December 25, 1991, after Gorbachev resigned, the red Soviet flag was taken down, marking the official end of the USSR. It was a quietly historic moment, watched live around the world.

11. **c) The Belavezha Accords** – Signed by leaders of Russia, Ukraine, and Belarus, it formally ended the USSR.

12. **c) Some weapons were left in former Soviet republics, creating security concerns** – Countries like Ukraine, Belarus, and Kazakhstan inherited nuclear weapons, but later gave them up.

13. **c) He stood on a tank and publicly defied the coup leaders** – This act made Yeltsin a national and global hero

14. **d) It had a confusing checkerboard pattern of land ownership at the border** – Though not directly caused by the USSR, Baarle became a metaphor for the post-Soviet border chaos, with its interlocking Dutch-Belgian plots. This complexity mirrored the difficulties of redrawing national boundaries peacefully.

15. **b) It led to ongoing tensions and conflicts over borders and political influence** – The Soviet collapse led to multiple conflicts, including Russia's annexation of Crimea and tensions in Georgia.

Future Predictions, Paradoxes, and Doomsdays

Throughout history, people have been fascinated—and sometimes terrified—by predictions about the future. From apocalyptic warnings that never came true to eerie forecasts that turned out to be strangely accurate, our past is filled with examples of prophecy, paranoia, and paradox. But how much of it was real, and how much was just human imagination running wild?

1. What was the primary fear behind the Y2K bug?
   a) That nuclear weapons would launch accidentally
   b) That computers would interpret the year 2000 as 1900 and fail globally
   c) That a computer virus would spread worldwide
   d) That a pandemic originating in bedbugs would sweep the globe

2. What did 19th-century fashion magazines predict about women's clothing in the year 2000?
   a) Floor-length smart-fabrics with built-in heaters
   b) Entirely metallic dresses
   c) Hover-enabled skirts
   d) Electric corsets controlled by radio

3. Which apocalyptic date, based on the Mayan calendar, caused global panic in 2012?
   a) October 31, 2012
   b) December 21, 2012
   c) January 1, 2013
   d) July 4, 2012

4. Which animated TV show famously predicted Donald Trump's presidency years before it happened?
   a) Family Guy
   b) South Park
   c) The Simpsons
   d) Futurama

5. Which of the following was *not* one of Nostradamus' supposed predictions?
   a) The rise of Napoleon
   b) The Great Fire of London
   c) The invention of the internet
   d) The assassination of John F. Kennedy

6. What did British civil engineer Sir John Sulman suggest in 1920 about cities of the future?
   a) That everyone would commute by underground tubes
   b) That cities would float in the sky
   c) That moving walkways would replace sidewalks
   d) That cars would be banned entirely in urban areas

7. Which failed prediction caused mass suicides when believers thought they would be taken to a spaceship behind a comet?
   a) The Hale-Bopp Comet prophecy
   b) The 2012 Mayan apocalypse
   c) The Nostradamus 1999 prophecy
   d) The CERN black hole theory

8. Which dystopian novel correctly predicted mass surveillance and government control?
   a) *Fahrenheit 451*
   b) *1984*
   c) *Brave New World*
   d) *The Handmaid's Tale*

9. What did the 16th-century monk Johannes Stöffler falsely predict would happen in 1524?
   a) A massive flood that would destroy the world
   b) The discovery of extraterrestrial life
   c) The end of the Catholic Church
   d) The invention of artificial intelligence

10. Which famous early 20th-century figure predicted that by the year 2000, people would be eating mostly food in pill form?
a) Jules Verne
b) Nikola Tesla
c) Winston Churchill
d) H.G. Wells

11. Which biblical prediction has been cited multiple times as evidence of an impending apocalypse?
a) The Four Horsemen of the Apocalypse
b) The Tower of Babel
c) The parting of the Red Sea
d) The flood of Noah

12. What major scientific discovery in the 20th century was once considered "impossible" but later reshaped human understanding?
a) The splitting of the atom
b) The discovery of gravity
c) The theory of relativity
d) The existence of germs

13. Which 19th-century book eerily predicted the sinking of the Titanic years before it happened?
a) *The Wreck of the Titan*
b) *20,000 Leagues Under the Sea*
c) *The Last Voyage*
d) *Into the Deep*

14. In 1955, what did science fiction author Robert Heinlein accurately predict about future society?
a) Widespread homeschooling via video
b) The collapse of gender roles in domestic work
c) The use of credit cards and electronic payments
d) The invention of online dating

15. What did Popular Mechanics boldly declare in 1949 about future computers?
    a) They would be able to think like humans
    b) They might become too small to maintain
    c) They would weigh no more than 1.5 tons
    d) They'd be household pets with personalities

ANSWERS

1. **b) That computers would interpret the year 2000 as 1900 and fail** – The Y2K bug was a fear that older computers would misread the date, potentially leading to major tech failures in vital systems across the globe. In reality, very few major incidents actually occurred.

2. **b) Entirely metallic dresses** – Some fashion illustrations from the late 19th century imagined women in futuristic, full-body metal outfits by 2000—practicality and comfort apparently not being a concern.

3. **b) December 21, 2012** – The Mayan calendar ended on this date, leading to widespread speculation about the end of the world.

4. **c) The Simpsons** – In a 2000 episode, *The Simpsons* joked that Trump would become president—a prediction that became reality in 2016.

5. **c) The invention of the internet** – While Nostradamus made many vague predictions, he never specifically mentioned the internet.

6. **c) That moving walkways would replace sidewalks** – Sulman envisioned vast "pavement conveyors" that would move pedestrians around cities. The idea didn't take off—except in airports.

7. **a) The Hale-Bopp Comet prophecy** – The Heaven's Gate cult believed a spaceship was hiding behind the comet and committed mass suicide in 1997.

8. **b) *1984*** – George Orwell's novel predicted government surveillance, propaganda, and mass control.
9. **a) A massive flood that would destroy the world** – Stöffler wrongly predicted a catastrophic flood based on planetary alignments.
10. **c) Winston Churchill** – In a 1931 essay, Churchill predicted that humans would eat synthetic meals in pill form, freeing time for higher pursuits. He was wrong, but he wasn't alone in thinking the future would be more efficient than delicious.
11. **a) The Four Horsemen of the Apocalypse** – Many believers see these figures as a warning of the end times.
12. **a) The splitting of the atom** – Once thought impossible, nuclear fission led to both nuclear power and atomic bombs.
13. **a) *The Wreck of the Titan*** – Published in 1898, this novel uncannily described a ship called *Titan* that sank after hitting an iceberg.
14. **c) The use of credit cards and electronic payments** – Heinlein, in his 1950s work, predicted credit-based transactions and digital finance, foreseeing a near-cashless society well before its time.
15. **C – They would weigh no more than 1.5 tons** – In 1949, *Popular Mechanics* said future computers might shrink to just 1.5 tons, suggesting that was an incredible leap in miniaturization. They didn't anticipate smartphones, obviously.

Final Score: How Did You Do?
- 60–75 correct: Historical Hero
- 45–59 correct: Seasoned Scholar
- 30–44 correct: Time-Travel Trainee
- 15–29 correct: Trivia Tourist
- 0–14 correct: Chronologically Confused

FINAL SHOWDOWN
The Ultimate Trivia Takedown Challenge

You've made it through the twists and turns of history, uncovering lost civilizations, bizarre historical events, and mind-blowing mysteries. Now, it's time for the ultimate test—100 of the toughest, most fascinating history questions to prove your mastery. Are you a **Casual Competitor**, a **History Buff**, or a true **Trivia Titan**? Let's begin!

Did you know...?

Napoleon was once attacked by a horde of bunnies. After a successful hunt was planned to celebrate a military victory, his men released hundreds of rabbits—but instead of running away, the tame creatures swarmed him. The organizers had mistakenly bought domesticated rabbits, who rushed Napoleon expecting food. The great general reportedly fled in laughter and confusion, outmaneuvered not by armies—but by fluffy, hungry adversaries.

1. Which ancient civilization is credited with creating the world's oldest surviving written legal code?
   a) The Romans
   b) The Babylonians
   c) The Sumerians
   d) The Egyptians

2. Which famous historical figure was never actually a ruler?
   a) Julius Caesar
   b) Cleopatra
   c) Genghis Khan
   d) Alexander the Great

3. Which ancient structure is older than the Great Pyramid of Giza?
   a) The Colosseum
   b) Stonehenge
   c) The Lighthouse of Alexandria
   d) The Great Wall of China

4. Which war is often called the first "modern war" due to its use of advanced weaponry and technology?
   a) The Napoleonic Wars
   b) The American Civil War
   c) World War I
   d) The Franco-Prussian War

5. Which ancient civilization is most famous for the legal principle of "an eye for an eye, a tooth for a tooth" (lex talionis) in its law code?
   a) The Assyrians
   b) The Babylonians
   c) The Egyptians
   d) The Hittites

6. What was the actual cause of the Great Fire of London in 1666?
   a) A lightning strike
   b) A bakery fire on Pudding Lane
   c) An explosion at a gunpowder warehouse
   d) A dropped lantern in St. Paul's Cathedral

7. Which empire was known for using an intricate network of knotted strings, called quipus, for record-keeping?
   a) The Mayan Empire
   b) The Roman Empire
   c) The Inca Empire
   d) The Ottoman Empire

8. Which country was NOT part of the Axis Powers during World War II?
   a) Japan
   b) Italy
   c) Spain
   d) Germany

9. Who was the first person to reach the South Pole?
   a) Robert Falcon Scott
   b) Roald Amundsen
   c) Ernest Shackleton
   d) Edmund Hillary

10. Which battle is considered the turning point of World War II in the Pacific?
    a) The Battle of Midway
    b) The Battle of Guadalcanal
    c) The Battle of Iwo Jima
    d) The Battle of the Coral Sea

11. What was the original purpose of the Leaning Tower of Pisa?
    a) A royal palace
    b) A military watchtower
    c) A church bell tower
    d) A lighthouse

12. Who was the last monarch of France before the French Revolution?
    a) Louis XIV
    b) Louis XVI
    c) Marie Antoinette
    d) Napoleon Bonaparte

13. Which event is considered the official start of the Cold War?
    a) The fall of the Berlin Wall
    b) The Cuban Missile Crisis
    c) The Truman Doctrine speech
    d) The construction of the Iron Curtain

14. Which city was the capital of the Eastern Roman Empire?
    a) Rome
    b) Constantinople
    c) Athens
    d) Carthage

15. Which scientist's theories led to the development of the atomic bomb?
    a) Albert Einstein
    b) Isaac Newton
    c) Nikola Tesla
    d) Marie Curie

16. Which ancient empire was the first to use a postal system?
    a) The Romans
    b) The Persians
    c) The Egyptians
    d) The Mongols

17. Which famous ship was discovered at the bottom of the Atlantic Ocean in 1985?
    a) The Bismarck
    b) The Lusitania
    c) The Titanic
    d) The Santa Maria

18. Which leader famously crossed the Alps with war elephants?
    a) Alexander the Great
    b) Julius Caesar
    c) Hannibal Barca
    d) Attila the Hun

19. Which of these U.S. presidents was NEVER assassinated?
    a) Abraham Lincoln
    b) James A. Garfield
    c) William McKinley
    d) Thomas Jefferson

20. Which war ended with the Treaty of Versailles?
    a) The Napoleonic Wars
    b) World War I
    c) World War II
    d) The Franco-Prussian War

21. What was the real reason the Colosseum in Rome was built?
    a) As a royal palace
    b) For religious ceremonies
    c) To entertain the public with gladiator fights
    d) As a military training ground

22. Who was the first woman to fly solo across the Atlantic Ocean?
    a) Bessie Coleman
    b) Amelia Earhart
    c) Valentina Tereshkova
    d) Harriet Quimby

23. In medieval China, what unusual material was sometimes used to make armor for elite soldiers?
    a) Silk
    b) Bamboo soaked in lacquer
    c) Fish scales
    d) Hardened paper

24. What was the Manhattan Project?
    a) A Cold War spy mission
    b) The codename for the Normandy landings
    c) The U.S. program to develop the atomic bomb
    d) A secret plan to assassinate Hitler

25. What did ancient Roman toilets lack that modern users would find essential?
    a) A flushing mechanism
    b) Dividers between seats
    c) Drainage systems
    d) Toilet paper

26. Which country was the first to land a spacecraft on the Moon?
    a) The United States
    b) The Soviet Union
    c) China
    d) France

27. What was the original purpose of the Great Wall of China?
    a) To block flooding from the Yellow River
    b) To protect China from northern invasions
    c) To act as a border between warring Chinese states
    d) To serve as a royal highway system

28. What unusual punishment was historically used in medieval Europe for counterfeiters and fraudsters?
    a) Branding with hot irons
    b) Having their hands cut off
    c) Being forced to wear a fool's cap in public
    d) Exile to a remote island

29. What event marked the end of the Middle Ages?
    a) The signing of the Magna Carta
    b) The fall of Constantinople
    c) The discovery of the Americas
    d) The Protestant Reformation

30. What is the name of the ship that rescued the majority of Titanic survivors in 1912?
    a) Carpathia
    b) Californian
    c) Birma
    d) Mount Temple

31. Which pharaoh's tomb was famously discovered almost completely intact in 1922?
    a) Ramses II
    b) Cleopatra VII
    c) Tutankhamun
    d) Akhenaten

32. Which U.S. state was an independent republic before joining the Union?
    a) Texas
    b) California
    c) Hawaii
    d) Vermont

33. Which empire created a 14,000-mile relay system of runners to send messages across mountainous terrain?
    a) Ottoman
    b) Mongol
    c) Inca
    d) Abbasid

34. What is the oldest known written story in human history?
    a) *The Iliad*
    b) *The Epic of Gilgamesh*
    c) *Beowulf*
    d) *The Aeneid*

35. What was banned in early 17th-century Japan as being "too indulgent and confusing"?
    a) Algebra
    b) Imported clocks
    c) Tobacco
    d) Sugar

36. Which medieval battle in 1066 changed the course of English history?
    a) The Battle of Agincourt
    b) The Battle of Hastings
    c) The Battle of Tours
    d) The Battle of Stirling Bridge

37. In the 19th century, Zanzibar briefly declared war on which European power, leading to the shortest war in history?
    a) France
    b) Germany
    c) Portugal
    d) Britain

38. What was the original name of the city of Istanbul before it was renamed in 1930?
    a) Byzantium
    b) Alexandria
    c) Constantinople
    d) Antioch

39. Who was the first U.S. president to resign from office?
    a) Richard Nixon
    b) Andrew Johnson
    c) Bill Clinton
    d) Herbert Hoover

40. Which empire was known for its elite warriors called the Janissaries?
    a) The Byzantine Empire
    b) The Ottoman Empire
    c) The Mongol Empire
    d) The Persian Empire

41. Which medieval European city required bakers to swear an oath not to *shrink their pies*?
    a) Paris
    b) Dublin
    c) London
    d) Florence

42. What surprising luxury item did ancient Mongols not give a currency-like function?
    a) Compressed cheese
    b) Strips of silk
    c) Sable pelts
    d) Tea bricks

43. Which country was the first to grant women the right to vote?
    a) The United States
    b) The United Kingdom
    c) New Zealand
    d) Sweden

44. Which language was used for many of the earliest English law books and statutes and later banned from English courts?
    a) Welsh
    b) Latin
    c) Cornish
    d) French

45. What was the primary goal of the Crusades?
    a) To establish European colonies in Africa
    b) To reclaim the Holy Land from Muslim rule
    c) To spread Christianity to the Americas
    d) To unite Europe under a single ruler

46. Which ancient empire was ruled by Cyrus the Great?
    a) Roman Empire
    b) Persian Empire
    c) Byzantine Empire
    d) Ottoman Empire

47. Who was the first man in space?
    a) Neil Armstrong
    b) Alan Shepard
    c) Yuri Gagarin
    d) Buzz Aldrin

48. Which war was sparked by the assassination of Archduke Franz Ferdinand?
    a) The Crimean War
    b) World War I
    c) The Franco-Prussian War
    d) World War II

49. What was the name of the Mongol leader who united the Mongol tribes and created the largest land empire at that time?
    a) Kublai Khan
    b) Attila the Hun
    c) Timur the Lame
    d) Genghis Khan

50. Which civilization is credited with creating the first known democracy?
    a) The Romans
    b) The Egyptians
    c) The Greeks
    d) The Mesopotamians

51. What odd item was often buried with Chinese scholars during the Han dynasty?
    a) Porcelain tea sets
    b) Wooden clocks
    c) Miniature libraries made of jade
    d) Replica servants carved in clay

52. In which country did people once pay a tax specifically for having *windows* in their homes?
    a) Italy
    b) France
    c) Britain
    d) Austria

53. Who was the longest-reigning monarch in British history?
    a) Queen Victoria
    b) King George III
    c) Queen Elizabeth I
    d) Queen Elizabeth II

54. Which city was the first to be targeted with an atomic bomb?
    a) Nagasaki
    b) Hiroshima
    c) Tokyo
    d) Kyoto

55. Who was the first emperor of China?
    a) Sun Tzu
    b) Wu Zetian
    c) Qin Shi Huang
    d) Kublai Khan

56. What unexpected profession did many Japanese samurai turn to during the peaceful Edo period?
    a) Butchers
    b) Postal workers
    c) Bureaucrats and accountants
    d) Opera singers

57. Which medieval king supposedly kept his crown jewels in pawn shops due to chronic financial troubles?
   a) King John of England
   b) Richard the Lionheart
   c) Henry VI
   d) Edward III

58. Which historical document begins with the words "When in the course of human events..."?
   a) The Magna Carta
   b) The U.S. Declaration of Independence
   c) The Communist Manifesto
   d) The Bill of Rights

59. Which ancient civilization built Machu Picchu?
   a) The Maya
   b) The Inca
   c) The Aztec
   d) The Olmec

60. Which country was responsible for building the Panama Canal after the French abandoned the project?
   a) The United Kingdom
   b) Spain
   c) The United States
   d) Brazil

61. Which notorious pirate was nicknamed "The Great Devil" by his terrified enemies?
   a) Edward Teach (Blackbeard)
   b) Bartholomew Roberts
   c) Zheng Yi Sao
   d) François l'Olonnais

62. Who was the last Tsar of Russia before the Russian Revolution?
   a) Alexander III
   b) Nicholas II
   c) Peter the Great
   d) Ivan the Terrible

63. What was the name of the ship that brought the Pilgrims to America in 1620?
    a) The Nina
    b) The Mayflower
    c) The Santa Maria
    d) The Endeavour

64. What did Victorian Britain ban in cemeteries to prevent alleged "moral corruption"?
    a) Statues of angels with bare feet
    b) Use of mirrors in mausoleums
    c) Picnicking on graves
    d) Curved tombstones

65. Which ancient city was destroyed by the eruption of Mount Vesuvius in 79 AD?
    a) Athens
    b) Carthage
    c) Pompeii
    d) Babylon

66. What was the primary cause of the War of the Roses in England?
    a) Religious conflict
    b) A dispute over the English throne
    c) Colonial expansion
    d) The Hundred Years' War

67. Who wrote the famous ancient military treatise *The Art of War*?
    a) Sun Tzu
    b) Confucius
    c) Julius Caesar
    d) Machiavelli

68. Which U.S. president issued the Emancipation Proclamation?
    a) George Washington
    b) Thomas Jefferson

c) Abraham Lincoln
d) Andrew Jackson

69. What strange innovation was used on some early 20th-century railways in India to reduce elephant collisions?
a) Hanging bells from locomotives
b) Painting trains to look like tigers
c) Installing pepper sprayers on the front
d) Using squeaky rubber tracks

70. What event marked the beginning of the Great Depression in the United States?
a) The Dust Bowl
b) The Stock Market Crash of 1929
c) The Prohibition Era
d) The New Deal

71. Which European nation, during the 18th century, banned coffeehouses for fear they would encourage revolution?
a) Austria
b) Sweden
c) France
d) Prussia

72. What bizarre method was once used in British factories to wake up child laborers who nodded off at work?
a) Cold water buckets
b) Spiked wheels
c) Nose twisters
d) Weighted "nodding straps"

73. What odd historical belief persisted into the 1800s about the cause of spontaneous human combustion?
a) Wearing wool too often
b) Drinking too much brandy
c) Eating spicy foods
d) Sleeping in metal beds

74. Who led the Soviet Union during the Cuban Missile Crisis?
    a) Joseph Stalin
    b) Vladimir Lenin
    c) Nikita Khrushchev
    d) Mikhail Gorbachev

75. Which famous document, signed in 1215, limited the power of the English monarchy?
    a) The Bill of Rights
    b) The Magna Carta
    c) The Declaration of Independence
    d) The Treaty of Versailles

76. Which 19th-century ruler ordered the construction of an entire city in the shape of a European chessboard?
    a) Napoleon Bonaparte
    b) Kamehameha I
    c) Haile Selassie
    d) King Ferdinand II of the Two Sicilies

77. What major world event is believed to have helped end the Great Depression?
    a) The discovery of penicillin
    b) World War II
    c) The Cold War
    d) The Korean War

78. Which European country was the first to establish a colony in what is now the United States?
    a) England
    b) Spain
    c) France
    d) The Netherlands

79. What famous event took place on July 20, 1969?
    a) The fall of the Berlin Wall
    b) The assassination of John F. Kennedy
    c) The first human landing on the Moon
    d) The launch of the first space station

80. Which empire was the largest in history by land area?
    a) The Roman Empire
    b) The Mongol Empire
    c) The British Empire
    d) The Ottoman Empire

81. Which 20th-century leader was known as the "Iron Lady"?
    a) Indira Gandhi
    b) Margaret Thatcher
    c) Angela Merkel
    d) Golda Meir

82. What was the main goal of the Marshall Plan?
    a) To rebuild Europe after World War II
    b) To stop the spread of communism in Asia
    c) To create a single European currency
    d) To establish the United Nations

83. The 17th-century Dutch tulip craze caused a single bulb to be traded for which of the following?
    a) A ship
    b) A townhouse
    c) A ton of cheese
    d) All of the above

84. The Mayan empire reportedly used what to stitch wounds?
    a) Gold thread
    b) Grass
    c) Spider's silk
    d) Ants

85. In 18th-century England, what were once popular ingredients in toothpaste?
    a) Gunpowder and crushed shells
    b) Bones and wood ash
    c) Sugar and spices
    d) Brick dust and burnt bread

86. Which battle is often considered Napoleon Bonaparte's final defeat?
    a) Battle of Austerlitz
    b) Battle of Leipzig
    c) Battle of Trafalgar
    d) Battle of Waterloo

87. What was the purpose of the Domesday Book, commissioned by William the Conqueror in 1086?
    a) To record English land ownership and taxation
    b) To document military victories
    c) To establish the feudal system
    d) To create an official English language

88. Which world leader was for a time obsessed with horoscopes, refusing to make key decisions without consulting his astrologer?
    a) Napoleon Bonaparte
    b) Adolf Hitler
    c) Benito Mussolini
    d) Franklin D. Roosevelt

89. Which African country successfully resisted European colonization in the 19th century?
    a) Nigeria
    b) Ethiopia
    c) Kenya
    d) South Africa

90. What unusual form of punishment was used by some Pacific Island societies to avoid bloodshed?
    a) Dance battles
    b) Song duels
    c) Staring contests
    d) Coconut duels

Final Round: The Ultimate 10 Questions (Super Hard – Double Points!)

You've battled through 90 questions, but now comes the real test. These last 10 questions are the most difficult yet, covering the most obscure, complex, and mind-bending pieces of history. If you can answer these, you're a true **Trivia Titan!**

---

91. What was the first recorded diplomatic treaty in history?
    a) The Treaty of Tordesillas
    b) The Peace of Westphalia
    c) The Treaty of Kadesh
    d) The Edict of Nantes

92. Which ancient civilization was the first known to use a system of underground aqueducts known as "qanats"?
    a) Roman
    b) Persian
    c) Egyptian
    d) Greek

93. Which country briefly had a king who ruled for just 20 minutes?
    a) Portugal
    b) Mexico
    c) France
    d) Italy

94. Who was the last ruler of the Western Roman Empire?
    a) Julius Nepos
    b) Romulus Augustulus
    c) Odoacer
    d) Theodosius I

95. Which empire was the first in history to stretch across three continents?
    a) The Macedonian Empire
    b) The Achaemenid Persian Empire

c) The Byzantine Empire
d) The Ottoman Empire

96. What was the real reason the Library of Alexandria was destroyed?
    a) Julius Caesar's fire during the Siege of Alexandria
    b) A Christian mob led by Theophilus
    c) The Muslim conquest in the 7th century
    d) It was never fully destroyed—books were gradually lost over time

97. What was the longest war in recorded history?
    a) The Hundred Years' War
    b) The Reconquista
    c) The Anglo-Zanzibar War
    d) The Three Hundred and Thirty-Five Years' War

98. What was the Enigma machine used for during World War II?
    a) Sending coded messages between Nazi officers
    b) Breaking Allied radio communications
    c) Tracking enemy aircraft movements
    d) Communicating between Soviet spies

99. Which historical event led directly to the formation of the modern banking system?
    a) The fall of Constantinople
    b) The Black Death
    c) The Medici family's rise in Florence
    d) The Industrial Revolution

100. Which territory remains the last on the United Nations' list of non-self-governing territories in Africa, with its decolonization process still officially unresolved since Spain withdrew in 1975?
    a) Namibia
    b) Chad
    c) East Timor
    d) Western Sahara

ANSWERS

1. **c) The Sumerians** – The Code of Ur-Nammu, written around 2100–2050 BCE, is the oldest known surviving legal code in history.

2. **a) Julius Caesar** – Despite his immense power, Caesar was never an emperor; he was declared "dictator for life" before being assassinated.

3. **b) Stonehenge** – Stonehenge dates back to around 3000 BCE, making it far older than the Great Pyramid, built in 2600 BCE.

4. **b) The American Civil War** – This war introduced rifled weapons, ironclad ships, and early versions of machine guns and submarines.

5. **b) The Babylonians** – The Code of Hammurabi, established by the Babylonian king Hammurabi around 1754 BCE, is renowned for its principle of lex talionis "an eye for an eye, a tooth for a tooth," which set the standard for retributive justice in the ancient world.

6. **b) A bakery fire on Pudding Lane** – The Great Fire of London started in a bakery and spread rapidly due to wooden buildings and strong winds.

7. **c) The Inca Empire** – The Incas used quipus, a system of knotted cords, to keep records in the absence of a written language.

8. **c) Spain** – Although led by the fascist dictator Francisco Franco, Spain remained officially neutral in World War II.

9. **b) Roald Amundsen** – The Norwegian explorer Amundsen was the first to reach the South Pole in 1911, beating the ill-fated British expedition of Robert Falcon Scott.

10. **a) The Battle of Midway** – This 1942 battle marked a decisive victory for the U.S. and a turning point in the Pacific War.

11. **c) A church bell tower** – The Leaning Tower of Pisa was built as a bell tower for the Pisa Cathedral but began tilting due to unstable ground.

12. **b) Louis XVI** – The last king before the French Revolution, he was executed by guillotine in 1793.

13. **c) The Truman Doctrine speech** – This 1947 speech marked the U.S. commitment to containing Soviet expansion, signaling the start of the Cold War.

14. **b) Constantinople** – The city, originally called Byzantium, became the capital of the Eastern Roman Empire and later the Ottoman Empire (modern-day Istanbul).

15. **a) Albert Einstein** – Einstein's $E=mc^2$ and his letter to Roosevelt led to the development of the atomic bomb through the Manhattan Project, but the bomb was developed by many scientists (notably Oppenheimer, Fermi, Szilard). Einstein did not work directly on the bomb.

16. **b) The Persians** – The Persian Empire, under King Darius I (circa 500 BCE), created one of the earliest postal systems called the "Chapar Khaneh."

17. **c) The Titanic** – The wreck of the Titanic was discovered in 1985, more than 70 years after it sank in 1912.

18. **c) Hannibal Barca** – The Carthaginian general famously led his army (including war elephants) across the Alps to attack Rome during the Second Punic War.

19. **d) Thomas Jefferson** – Unlike Lincoln, Garfield, and McKinley, Jefferson died of natural causes.

20. **b) World War I** – The Treaty of Versailles was signed in 1919, formally ending World War I and placing heavy penalties on Germany.

21. **c) To entertain the public with gladiator fights** – The Colosseum was a massive arena built in 80 CE for

public spectacles, including gladiator battles and mock sea battles.

22. **b) Amelia Earhart** – In 1932, she became the first woman to fly solo across the Atlantic, though she later disappeared on her attempted world flight.

23. **a) Silk** – Silk armor was real—it could absorb and slow arrows, especially from traditional weapons like those of the Mongols.

24. **c) The U.S. program to develop the atomic bomb** – The Manhattan Project (1942-1945) resulted in the creation of the first nuclear weapons, which were later used in Hiroshima and Nagasaki.

25. **d) Toilet paper** – Romans used shared sponges on sticks, rinsed in communal buckets—sanitary standards have, thankfully, evolved.

26. **b) The Soviet Union** – The USSR was the first to land a spacecraft on the Moon in 1959 with Luna 2, although the U.S. was the first to put humans on the Moon in 1969.

27. **b) To protect China from northern invasions** – The Great Wall was built to defend against invasions from Mongol and other nomadic tribes.

28. **b) Having their hands cut off** – In medieval Europe, counterfeiters and fraudsters were often punished severely to deter crime. One common punishment was amputation of the hands, symbolizing the removal of the ability to commit further fraud.

29. **b) The fall of Constantinople** – The capture of Constantinople by the Ottoman Empire in 1453 marked the end of the Middle Ages and the start of the Renaissance.

30. **a) Carpathia** – The RMS Carpathia arrived at the scene after the Titanic sank and rescued over 700 survivors from lifeboats.

31. **c) Tutankhamun** – Howard Carter discovered King Tut's tomb in 1922, making it one of the most significant archaeological finds of the 20th century.

32. **a) Texas** – Texas was an independent republic from 1836 to 1845 before becoming the 28th U.S. state.

33. **c) Inca** – The Inca used chasquis—relay runners who could carry quipu (knot-writing) messages across thousands of miles in a few days.

34. **b) *The Epic of Gilgamesh*** – Written around 2100 BCE in Mesopotamia, it is the oldest known literary work.

35. **c) Tobacco** – Tobacco was briefly banned under the Tokugawa shogunate as both decadent and foreign.

36. **b) The Battle of Hastings** – In 1066, William the Conqueror defeated King Harold II, leading to the Norman conquest of England.

37. **d) Britain** – The 1896 Anglo-Zanzibar War lasted only 38 minutes—shortest war in recorded history.

38. **c) Constantinople** – Originally called Byzantium, the city was renamed Constantinople in 330 CE before becoming Istanbul in 1930.

39. **a) Richard Nixon** – Nixon resigned in 1974 due to the Watergate scandal, making him the only U.S. president to resign.

40. **b) The Ottoman Empire** – The Janissaries were elite Ottoman soldiers, known for their discipline and loyalty to the sultan.

41. **c) London** – Guilds in medieval London required pie bakers to uphold strict size and content standards. Shrinking pies could mean a fine.

42. **a) Compressed cheese** –Tea bricks, sable pelts, and strips of silk all had a currency-like function or were used as high-value barter items in Mongol-controlled regions.

43. **c) New Zealand** – In 1893, New Zealand became the first country to grant women the right to vote in national elections.

44. **d) French** – After the Norman Conquest, Anglo-Norman (Law French) became the language of English law and legal documents. It remained in use for statutes and court proceedings for centuries, until the Statute of Pleading (1362) and later acts required English instead.

45. **b) To reclaim the Holy Land from Muslim rule** – The Crusades were a series of religious wars between Christians and Muslims, primarily focused on the Holy Land.

46. **b) Persian Empire** – Cyrus the Great founded the Persian Empire around 550 BCE and is remembered for his military leadership and progressive policies.

47. **c) Yuri Gagarin** – The Soviet cosmonaut became the first human in space on April 12, 1961.

48. **b) World War I** – The assassination of Archduke Franz Ferdinand of Austria in 1914 triggered a global conflict.

49. **d) Genghis Khan** – Genghis Khan united the Mongol tribes and established the Mongol Empire, which stretched from China to Europe.

50. **c) The Greeks** – Athens is credited with developing the first form of democracy around 500 BCE.

51. **d) Replica servants carved in clay** – These "mingqi" objects symbolized servants for the afterlife and were commonly buried with scholars and nobles.

52. **c) Britain** – The "window tax" (1696–1851) made windows a luxury, which is why many old British homes have bricked-up window spaces.

53. **d) Queen Elizabeth II** – She reigned from 1952 to 2022, making her the longest-reigning British monarch.

54. **b) Hiroshima** – The first atomic bomb was dropped on Hiroshima, Japan, on August 6, 1945.

55. **c) Qin Shi Huang** – He unified China in 221 BCE and built the first version of the Great Wall.

56. **c) Bureaucrats and accountants** – During the peaceful Edo period, many samurai had no battles to fight and turned to administrative roles in Japan's growing civil system.

57. **d) Edward III** – He had such severe cash flow issues that he famously pawned the crown jewels to pay for his campaigns during the Hundred Years' War.

58. **b) The U.S. Declaration of Independence** – Written in 1776, this document declared the American colonies' separation from Britain.

59. **b) The Inca** – Machu Picchu, an architectural marvel, was built by the Inca Empire in present-day Peru.

60. **c) The United States** – After the French failed to complete the canal, the U.S. took over construction and finished it in 1914.

61. **d) François l'Olonnais** – This fearsome French pirate terrorized the Caribbean in the 17th century.

62. **b) Nicholas II** – The last Tsar of Russia was overthrown during the Russian Revolution in 1917 and later executed with his family.

63. **b) The Mayflower** – The Pilgrims traveled from England to America aboard the Mayflower in 1620, establishing Plymouth Colony.

64. **c) Picnicking on graves** – In the 1800s, it was common for families to picnic in cemeteries. Victorian reforms discouraged this, fearing it encouraged "unseemly behavior."

65. **c) Pompeii** – The ancient Roman city of Pompeii was buried under volcanic ash when Mount Vesuvius erupted in 79 AD.

66. **b) A dispute over the English throne** – The War of the Roses (1455–1487) was a civil war between the rival Houses of Lancaster and York.

67. **a) Sun Tzu** – The Chinese military strategist wrote *The Art of War* in the 5th century BCE, and it is still studied today.

68. **c) Abraham Lincoln** – Lincoln issued the Emancipation Proclamation in 1863, declaring that enslaved people in Confederate states were free.

69. **a) Hanging bells from locomotives** – The most historically documented method was hanging bells from locomotives to scare elephants. Painting trains like tigers is a popular myth but not supported by railway records.

70. **b) The Stock Market Crash of 1929** – The Wall Street crash in October 1929 triggered the Great Depression, an economic crisis that lasted for years.

71. **b) Sweden** – In 1746, coffee was banned in Sweden due to fears of "excessive stimulation and intellectual plotting" in coffeehouses.

72. **d) Weighted "nodding straps"** – Children wore straps with weights; if they nodded off, the weight would swing forward and hit their heads—an industrial-era horror.

73. **b) Drinking too much brandy** – Spontaneous human combustion was blamed on overconsumption of alcohol—especially brandy—based on a few odd, fiery deaths.

74. **c) Nikita Khrushchev** – The Soviet leader negotiated with U.S. President John F. Kennedy to de-escalate the Cuban Missile Crisis in 1962.

75. **b) The Magna Carta** – Signed in 1215, this document forced King John of England to limit his power and recognize certain legal rights.

76. **d) King Ferdinand II of the Two Sicilies** – Ferdinand II designed the city of Ferdinandia (now known as Ferdinandea) in a perfect chessboard layout.

77. **b) World War II** – The war effort led to massive economic growth, helping countries recover from the Great Depression.

78. **b) Spain** – Spain established the first European colony in what is now the U.S. at St. Augustine, Florida, in 1565.

79. **c) The first human landing on the Moon** – On July 20, 1969, Apollo 11's Neil Armstrong became the first human to set foot on the Moon.

80. **c) The British Empire** – At its peak, the British Empire controlled about 25% of the world's land area.

81. **b) Margaret Thatcher** – The former British Prime Minister earned the nickname "Iron Lady" for her strong policies and controversial leadership style.

82. **a) To rebuild Europe after World War II** – The Marshall Plan provided economic aid to help rebuild war-torn European nations.

83. **d) All of the above** – Tulip mania was so extreme that rare bulbs were traded for houses, ships, and tons of goods, sparking one of history's first speculative bubbles.

84. **d) Mayan** – Soldier ants were used by the Maya; they'd clamp their jaws on a wound, and their bodies would be snipped off, acting like surgical staples.

85. **d) Brick dust and burnt bread** – Brick dust and burnt breadcrumbs were used in early toothpaste for their abrasive qualities—though not great for enamel.

86. **d) Battle of Waterloo** – Napoleon was defeated at Waterloo in 1815 by a coalition of European forces.

87. **a) To record English land ownership and taxation** – The Domesday Book was a detailed census of England, used for taxation purposes.

88. **b) Adolf Hitler** – Hitler regularly consulted astrologers and made several military decisions based on astrological advice—until he turned against them later in the war.

89. **b) Ethiopia** – Ethiopia successfully resisted Italian colonization at the Battle of Adwa in 1896.

90. **b) Song duels** – In some Inuit and Pacific cultures, disputes were settled through insult-laden song duels—avoiding violence and entertaining communities.

91. **c) The Treaty of Kadesh** – Signed in 1259 BCE between the Egyptians and Hittites, this is the oldest surviving peace treaty in history.

92. **b) Persian** – Qanats were a clever system of underground channels to transport water from aquifers to the surface, which enabled agriculture and settlements to flourish in arid regions.

93. **c) France** – King Louis XIX of France ruled for just 20 minutes in 1830 before abdicating. Italy's candidate for shortest reign would be Umberto II, who ruled for just over a month.

94. **b) Romulus Augustulus** – Deposed in 476 CE, he was the last emperor of the Western Roman Empire.

95. **b) The Achaemenid Persian Empire** – Under Cyrus the Great, Persia became the first empire to span Asia, Africa, and Europe.

96. **d) It was never fully destroyed—books were gradually lost over time** – The Library of Alexandria suffered multiple incidents of destruction, but no single event wiped it out completely.

97. **b) The Reconquista** – This conflict between Christian and Muslim forces in Spain lasted **781 years** (711–1492).

98. **a) Sending coded messages between Nazi officers** – The Enigma machine encrypted German military communications, until Alan Turing and his team cracked the code.

99. **c) The Medici family's rise in Florence** – The Medici introduced early forms of modern banking in Renaissance Italy, including double-entry bookkeeping.

100. **d) Western Sahara** – Spain relinquished control in 1975, but the territory's final status remains unresolved, making it the last African territory still awaiting a completed decolonization process.

Final Score – How Did You Do?

Now that you've battled through 100 mind-bending history questions, it's time to see where you rank among the history elite! Each question was worth **1 point**, except for the **final 10 ultra-hard questions, which were worth double points**—meaning the maximum score is **110 points**. Check your score below and claim your title!

0-35 Points: Casual Competitor

You enjoy history, but let's be honest—maybe you weren't taking notes along the way! You might know the big events and famous figures, but those obscure details? Not quite in your wheelhouse. No worries—history is vast and fascinating, and this challenge was designed to be tough. Keep learning, stay curious, and next time, you might just climb to the next level!

36-70 Points: History Buff

You've got a solid grasp of history and probably wow your friends with random facts at parties. You know your revolutions from your renaissances, and you can confidently discuss world history beyond just the basics. However, some of those ultra-hard questions might have tripped you up—especially the obscure treaties, ancient texts, or forgotten conflicts.

71-110 Points: Trivia Titan

Welcome to the elite ranks of historical masterminds! You didn't just pass this challenge—you dominated it. You know the names, the dates, the obscure treaties, and even the forgotten details of history that most people overlook. Whether you're a lifelong history enthusiast, a trivia champion, or just someone with an incredible memory, you've proven yourself as a top-tier history expert.

You can debate historical inaccuracies in movies, explain why certain wars started, and probably predict which future historical discoveries will rewrite our textbooks. If history had a Hall of Fame, your name would be in it!

Final Words: The Never-Ending Puzzle of History

History is a puzzle with no final piece. Just when we think the big picture is complete, a new discovery—a lost manuscript, a buried ruin, a declassified file—reshapes everything we thought we knew. Far from being static, history is constantly rewritten, challenged, and reimagined. It's a living narrative, evolving with each fresh perspective, unanswered question, or unexpected find.

What keeps us hooked? It's not just what we know—it's what we *don't*. From the fate of the Mary Celeste's crew to the secrets of Atlantis or the true extent of Cold War espionage, the mysteries of the past spark curiosity. These open questions drive historians, researchers, and everyday sleuths to keep digging. The unknown makes history feel alive, urgent, and deeply human.

And history isn't just global—it's personal. Our identities, cultures, and stories are tied to it. That's why trivia about history matters. It's not just entertainment; it's a way of preserving the obscure, the strange, and the forgotten stories that make up our collective past.

Too often, we remember only the big moments—battles, kings, revolutions. But the past is also shaped by everyday people, strange customs, and minor events that ripple through time. Trivia and lesser-known facts help preserve this richness. They invite us to ask deeper questions: Whose stories were left out? What overlooked moments quietly shaped the world?

Studying history isn't just about the past—it helps us understand the present and shape the future. Patterns repeat. Decisions echo. Propaganda, power struggles, and political maneuvering from centuries ago still offer lessons today. Knowing what came before makes us more informed citizens and better decision-makers. History is a map, not just a record.

Perhaps the greatest gift of history is its ability to challenge what we think we know. Many once-radical ideas—heliocentrism, women's suffrage, the complexity of ancient civilizations—were eventually proven true. This teaches us to question received wisdom, remain open to new evidence, and never assume the story is over.

An Open Invitation

History is still unfolding. Lost cities are being found by satellite. DNA tests are rewriting ancestry. New tools, from AI to archaeology, are pushing boundaries every day. So, ask questions, challenge what you're told, and keep exploring. Whether you scored high in the quiz or simply learned something new, remember: being curious is the true mark of a history lover.

Keep questioning. Keep exploring. And most of all—keep making history.

Want More?

Did you enjoy Ultimate Trivia Takedown Challenge and want some more intriguing trivia?

Get yours at WWW.ROBINWHY.COM

Your Review Matters

I'm immensely grateful for your support in choosing this book! If you enjoyed the read, could you please take a moment to leave a review on Amazon? Your feedback is vital, especially for self-published authors. You will help me reach more readers and continue creating books you love. Thank you for being part of my literary journey!

Click on your link below to be taken straight to my Amazon book review page...

US	geni.us/ultimatehistoryUSpb
UK	geni.us/ultimatehistoryUKpb
AUS	geni.us/ultimatehistoryAUpb
CA	geni.us/ultimatehistoryCApb

I'm excited to read your thoughts!

About the Author

Hello, nice to meet you. I'm Robin Why. I like to travel to the far corners of this planet, gathering facts to build my towering nest of knowledge.

With a nose for prose, I'm often found lost in a book, exploring the vast literary landscapes and seeking inspiration for my next project.

When not writing, I also enjoy discovering new horizons, novel activities, and intriguing cultures, seeking out the all the weird and wonderful experiences that this world has to offer.

My obsession with humanity took flight when I discovered just how wonderfully diverse people are. They never fail to amaze me.

So, dear curiosity-seekers, I welcome you to get comfy and settle down for an excellent read. I'm here to take your mind on a journey like no other.

Sign up to Robin's newsletter to receive a free book, updates, and the latest releases at:

WWW.ROBINWHY.COM

More Books by Robin Why

The Trivia Book of Wow

How did a message in a bottle save the lives of 80 people?
Where were the world's most valuable treasures found?
What does it mean to be a superhuman runner?
How can a jellyfish be immortal?

Get ready for a mysterious, and mind-bending journey with the **Trivia Book of Wow**, the ULTIMATE fact book.

1,369 Fascinating Factoids
Whether you're a lifelong trivia-lover or a budding young factologist, this book is the perfect companion for inquisitive souls. Both educating and entertaining, each page is bursting with hilarious and outlandish titbits of information to ignite your curiosity.

The Random and the Riveting
From astonishing animals to gobsmacking galaxies, you'll find countless pearls of wisdom, ready to stun the next person who walks in the room!

The ultimate gift for kids who are ready to be WOWed.

The Free Life Revolution

Welcome to part one of The Free Life Revolution – an invitation to rediscover the power and potential that resides within you, through practices that are both ancient and innovative, simple yet profoundly transformative.

Whether you're new to the concept of holistic health or a seasoned practitioner seeking fresh insights, this journey is designed for everyone, no matter where you're starting from or what resources you have.

In these pages, you'll find practical, zero-cost strategies to help you nourish your body, calm your mind, and reignite your spirit.

In your hands is a roadmap to a life brimming with energy, clarity, and a deep connection to both yourself and the planet around you.

So, are you ready to revolutionise your life? Let's begin.

geni.us/liferevolution

The Free Life Revolution
Book 2

What if the world were your playground, adventure your currency, and the sky your limit? The second part of the *Free Life Revolution* is here to show you that freedom, joy, and growth don't come with a price tag – they come with boldness, creativity, and the willingness to see things differently.

Cultivate a New Money Mindset by choosing self-reliance and decluttering life.
Find the Antidote to Loneliness through new connections and exhilarating hobbies.
Break Free from the Ordinary *without* breaking the bank.

Packed with practical strategies, zero-cost hacks and thrilling possibilities, this guide will inspire you to break out of your shell and reach your full potential.

Adventure is out there, and it's calling your name.

geni.us/liferevolution2

Stay in the Loop

Did you enjoy this book? Keep up-to-date with the release of new books by joining the mailing list.

WWW.ROBINWHY.COM

Free Trivia Audiobook

Sign up to Audible and use your free credit to download the *Trivia Book of Wow*. If you cancel within 30 days, there's no charge!

WWW.ROBINWHY.COM/FREE-AUDIOBOOK

★★★★★

'This book made my heart happy... interesting, perplexing, funny, eye-opening and a whole lot of fun to read.'
–Dr. Eric Trevizu
'Purchased for a long car ride. Worth the money! Fun facts that keep kids busy!'
–L. Nichols
'Filled with really interesting facts, figures, stories...'
–Alan R. Vance
'This was a gift for my 87-year-old dad. He loved all the information...'
–VJ
As an adult I enjoyed the facts but it would also be suitable for children. It's a good learning tool.
–Tiaf

WWW.ROBINWHY.COM/FREE-AUDIOBOOK